The BakerStreet Four, Vol. 2

The BakerStreet Four, Vol. 2

Written by **J. B. DJIAN and OLIVIER LEGRAND**

Art by **DAVID ETIEN**

San Rafael, California

The Stepney Nightingale

"It is the unofficial force,
the Baker Street Irregulars."
— Sherlock Holmes

ARTHUR CONAN DOYLE,
The Sign of the Four

HAVE MERCY! I'M BEGGIN' YA... I JUST NEED A FEW MORE DAYS...

TIMES ARE HARD AND--

I THOUGHT I MADE MYSELF CLEAR, YOU OLD NAG! MR. SYKES'S HOUSE DOESN'T OFFER CREDIT, AND YOU'RE THREE WEEKS OVERDUE...

...SO NOW IT'S TIME TO PAY UP.

STOP! I... I WILL PAY!

OF COURSE YOU'LL PAY! AND DON'T GO THINKING WE'LL LET YOU OFF THE INTEREST!

CRUSHER, WOULD YOU EXPLAIN THE RULES OF THE GAME TO OUR FRIEND?

YOU VILLAINS! LEAVE MY FATHER ALONE!

WELL! WE'VE UPSET THE STEPNEY NIGHTINGALE!

ANGER JUST DOESN'T BECOME YOU, MY LOVELY...

CLACK

ENOUGH, CRUSHER! IF YOU GO ON, OUR FRIEND MIGHT GIVE UP THE GHOST.

OLD PEOPLE ARE SO FRAGILE...

LISTEN HERE, YOU OLD WRECK...

YOU HAVE THREE DAYS TO PAY YOUR DUES TO MISTER SYKES... AND YOU CAN ADD A QUARTER ON TOP FOR BEING LATE.

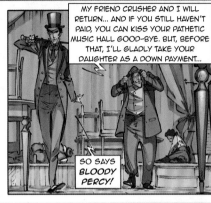

MY FRIEND CRUSHER AND I WILL RETURN... AND IF YOU STILL HAVEN'T PAID, YOU CAN KISS YOUR PATHETIC MUSIC HALL GOOD-BYE. BUT, BEFORE THAT, I'LL GLADLY TAKE YOUR DAUGHTER AS A DOWN PAYMENT...

SO SAYS BLOODY PERCY!

"GRACE! OH GRACE, ME DARLIN'... WE NEED... YOU HAVE TO... WE'RE DOOMED!"

NO, FATHER, THERE MUST BE A WAY! WE SHOULD GO TO THE POLICE AND...

NO! THAT'S WHAT OL' MAN STEPHENSON DONE! LOOK WHAT HAPPENED TO HIM...

SYKES BRIBES THE POLICE. DON'T YA SEE? HE'LL FIND OUT IN NO TIME, AND THEN...

I COULD TALK TO THE YOUNG GENTLEMAN WHO COMES TO HEAR ME SING EVERY NIGHT. HE MUST HAVE FRIENDS IN HIGH PLACES!

IF I TELL HIM OUR TROUBLES, HE MIGHT AGREE TO HELP US OUT. HE SEEMS TO BE RICH AND...SO NOBLE.

YES, PERHAPS I COULD...

HIS NAME IS *LORD NEVILLE ASPREY* THE THIRD, AND HE IS 19 YEARS OLD.

HAVING RECENTLY INHERITED HIS LATE FATHER'S TITLE, THE YOUNG GENTLEMAN IS NOW IN THE HABIT OF SLUMMING IN THE EAST END ALMOST EVERY EVENING.

INCOGNITO, OF COURSE... MUCH TO THE CHAGRIN OF HIS MOTHER, *LADY ANTONIA*.

WORRIED ABOUT HIS FUTURE AND ANXIOUS TO HUSH UP ANY POTENTIAL SCANDALS, SHE ASKED ME TO INVESTIGATE HIS NOCTURNAL ESCAPADES.

I DIDN'T HAVE THE HEART TO REFUSE HER THIS LITTLE FAVOR...

BUT I'M CURRENTLY IN PURSUIT OF SOME FAR MORE INTERESTING PREY!

HAVE YOU HEARD OF *PROFESSOR MORIARTY?*

ER... NO, SIR...

HE IS THE NAPOLEON OF CRIME, BILLY FLETCHER!

AT LAST, AN ADVERSARY WHO IS A MATCH FOR ME! WE ARE ENGAGED IN A VERITABLE CHESS GAME, WITH LONDON AS OUR CHESSBOARD...

AND I FULLY INTEND TO CHECKMATE HIM!

THEREFORE, I HAVE NO TIME TO WASTE ON TRIFLES SUCH AS LORD NEVILLE ASPREY'S ANTICS OR HIS DEAR LADY MOTHER'S FEARS...

SO I NEED COMPETENT ASSISTANTS NOW MORE THAN EVER, MY YOUNG FRIENDS!

ESPECIALLY SINCE THAT COWARD, WATSON, HAS DESERTED BAKER STREET, ENTICED BY THE SIRENS OF DOMESTIC BLISS...

BUT BACK TO OUR CASE!

AFTER A BRIEF INVESTIGATION, I DISCOVERED THAT LORD NEVILLE VISITS A THIRD-RATE EAST-END MUSIC HALL, THE MERRY MINSTREL, EVERY EVENING.

YOUR MISSION WILL BE TO GO THERE AND OBSERVE HIS LORDSHIP, HIS ACTIVITIES, AND THE COMPANY HE KEEPS.

OH, I ALMOST FORGOT: HERE IS A PHOTOGRAPH OF HIS LORDSHIP...

...AND SOMETHING TO COVER ANY EXPENSES YOU MAY INCUR.

ANY QUESTIONS? NO? PERFECT! I SHALL EXPECT YOUR REPORT IN THREE DAYS!

AS FOR ME, I MUST ATTEND A MEETING OF THE UTMOST IMPORTANCE. THE GAME IS AFOOT!

MRS. HUDSON! MAKE SURE OUR YOUNG FRIENDS TAKE EXTRA SUPPLIES OF THAT DELICIOUS CAKE OF YOURS WITH THEM!

HERE I COME, PROFESSOR MORIARTY!

DON'T OVERDO IT NOW, BILLY FLETCHER...

?

WHAT'S A MENTOR?

HAS HE LOST HIS MIND, OR WHAT?!

DOESN'T MATTER! OUR MENTOR'S GIVEN US A MISSION. HE'S COUNTING ON OUR EFFICIENCY. *BAKER STREET IRREGULARS, LET'S BE OFF!*

CLAP

P'RAPS HE REALLY DOES NEED THE DOCTOR FOR ONCE? WHO IS THIS PROFESSOR WHATSHISNAME, ANYWAY?

SO HOW'S OUR BUSINESS DOIN'?

CRUSHER TELLS ME YA GAVE OL' CORBETT THREE MORE DAYS... SO GENEROUS O' YA! D'YA REALLY THINK HE'LL RAISE THE CASH BY THEN?

NO CHANCE, HARRY! I JUST FANCIED A BIT OF FUN, LETTING HIM BELIEVE HE HAS HOPE BEFORE WE PASS SENTENCE.

HIS PLACE HAS STOPPED MAKIN' MONEY, ANYHOW. TAKE CARE OF IT TONIGHT!

CORBETT NEEDS A LESSON, AND THE DISTRICT NEEDS AN EXAMPLE.

THAT'S THE PLAN. SCABS AND SCRUFFY WILL HANDLE IT TONIGHT. BUT, BEFORE THAT, I'LL PAY A SURPRISE VISIT TO CORBETT'S DAUGHTER, IF YOU KNOW WHAT I MEAN...

WOMEN'LL BE THE DEATH O' YA, PERCY. NO MESSIN' AROUND TONIGHT. TAKE CARE O' THE MINSTREL FIRST, GOT IT?

YOU CAN ALWAYS MUCK ABOUT WITH THE GIRL AFTERWARD...IF THERE'S ANYTHIN' LEFT OF HER. IT'S A MATTER O' PRIORITIES.

IN BUSINESS, IT'S ALL A MATTER O' PRIORITIES.

NEVILLE!

ARE YOU GOING OUT?

YES, MOTHER. I SWEAR, I CAN'T HIDE A THING FROM YOU!

I KNOW WHERE YOU ARE GOING, NEVILLE. I WILL NOT ALLOW YOU TO DISHONOR YOUR LATE FATHER'S NAME LIKE THIS!

I'M NOT DISHONORING ANYTHING, MOTHER!

IN CASE YOU'VE FORGOTTEN, I'M OLD ENOUGH TO GO WHEREVER I PLEASE, MEET WHOEVER I WANT, AND SPEND MY MONEY HOWEVER I WISH. AND NOW--

YOU'RE WRONG, MY SON!

THE FAMILY COUNCIL? WHAT FOR?

DO YOU HONESTLY BELIEVE THAT SIR CHARLES WILL ALLOW YOU TO SQUANDER THE FAMILY FORTUNE IN THE ARMS OF...LOOSE WOMEN?

I DON'T GO THERE FOR THE RIFFRAFF, MOTHER! I'M IN LOVE! CAN'T YOU UNDERSTAND THAT?

YOUR UNCLE, *SIR CHARLES*, HAS INSINUATED THAT HE WILL CONVENE THE FAMILY COUNCIL IF YOU DON'T PUT A STOP TO YOUR MISCHIEF. FOR THE LOVE OF GOD AND ENGLAND, NEVILLE...

NO... I DON'T SUPPOSE YOU CAN...

MY UNCLE SHOULD TAKE CARE OF HIS MISTRESSES INSTEAD!

NEVILLE! HOW DARE YOU!

GOOD NIGHT, MOTHER!

IN LOVE?! WITH...ONE OF THOSE...CREATURES FROM THE EAST END? MY GOD, IT'S EVEN WORSE THAN I HAD IMAGINED. YOU MUST ABANDON SUCH FOOLHARDY IDEAS AT ONCE! SIR CHARLES WILL NEVER ALLOW YOU TO--

NEVILLE, COME BACK! NEVILLE, I BEG OF YOU...

GOD, THIS DUMP IS TERRIBLE.

THAT'S IT, MY FRIENDS, I'VE SPOTTED OUR SUBJECT.

NO KIDDIN'? HIS LORDSHIP STICKS OUT A MILE, NO PHOTOGRAPH NEEDED! YOU'DA NOTICED HIM BEFORE IF YA WEREN'T SO BUSY LOOKIN' AWAY, TRYIN' TO ACT ALL NATURAL-LIKE...

EXCUSE ME FOR TRYING NOT TO BE SPOTTED!

YEAH, WELL YOU'RE ABOUT AS NATURAL AS *HE* IS...

A BIG ROUND OF APPLAUSE FOR THE INIMITABLE *TOBY TINKLE!* THREE CHEERS FOR TOBY!

AND NOW, LADIES AND GENTLEMEN...

CLAP CLAP

YA SEE THAT GEEZER'S FACE? LOOKS LIKE SOMEONE GAVE HIM A REAL THRASHIN'.

LAST NIGHT'S CUSTOMERS, I'LL BET.

SHH! LOOK AT HIS LORDSHIP!

...IT'S MY PLEASURE TO INTRODUCE THE STEPNEY NIGHTINGALE; THE CANARY O' THE EAST END...

MISS *GRACE CORBETT!*

LADIES AND GENTLEMEN, TONIGHT I WILL SING YOU A SONG THAT'S DEAR TO MY HEART...

♫ OH! LET ME DREAM OF HAPPY DAYS GONE BY, FORGETTING SORROWS THAT HAVE COME BETWEEN... ♫

♫ IN YOUTH, WE PLUCKED FULL MANY A FLOWER THAT DIED... ♫

♫ DROPPED ON THE PATHWAY, AS WE DANCED ALONG... ♫

♫ WHEN ALL THE FIRES OF LIFE ARE DEAD... OH! LET ME DREAM OF HAPPY DAYS GONE BY... ♫

THE GAL'S GOT A LOVELY LITTLE VOICE!

YEAH, IT GETS YA RIGHT THERE!

RUN FOR YER LIVES!

HELP! HELP!

LET ME THROUGH!

YOU'RE STAYIN' WITH ME!

HURRY UP!

I CAN'T SEE LORD NEVILLE... I THINK HE'S BACK THERE!

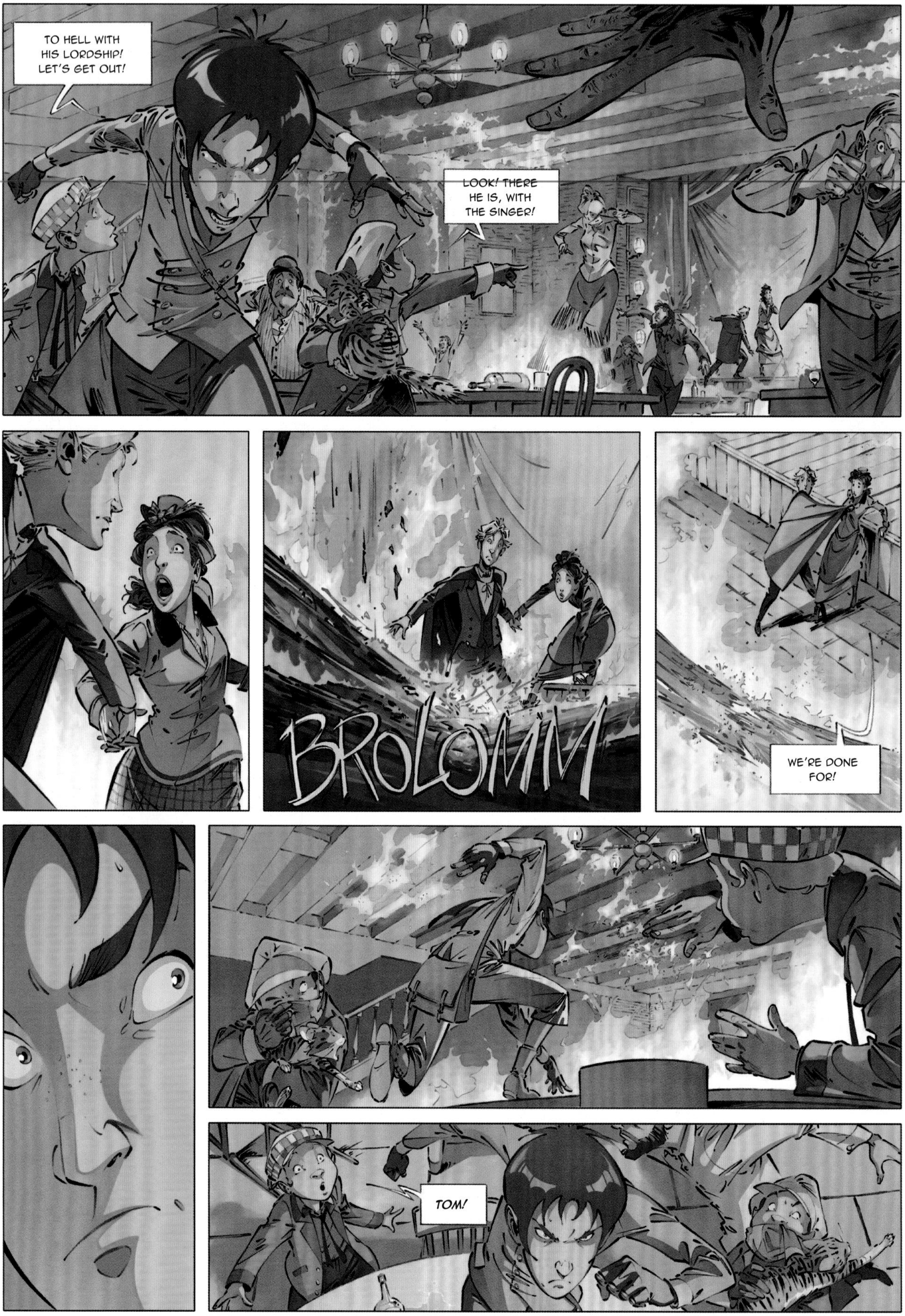

TO HELL WITH HIS LORDSHIP! LET'S GET OUT!
LOOK! THERE HE IS, WITH THE SINGER!
BROLOMM
WE'RE DONE FOR!
TOM!

WATSON!

CHARLIE!

HELP ME CARRY HER! WE'LL TAKE THE STAIRS!

COUGH COUGH

YOU'RE MAD! THE FLAMES...

DON'T ARGUE, YA TOFF! WANNA BE ROASTED ALIVE?

DON'T MOVE, WATSON... GOOD KITTY...

CHARLOTTE!!!

CHARLIE! CHARLIE!

GOOD TIMIN', BILLY FLETCHER!

15

CHARLIE'S GONE UP THERE TO GET HER STUPID CAT BACK!

HELP ME INSTEAD O' TALKIN' RUBBISH!

WE CAN GET ONTO THE ROOF OUTTA THE WINDOW! MOVE!

WE'RE ALL GOING TO DIE!

FATHER! FATHER!

YOUR FATHER REQUIRES URGENT TREATMENT, MISS! WE NEED TO TAKE HIM TO HOSPITAL!

MY FRIENDS, I OWE YOU MY LIFE... NOT TO MENTION THE YOUNG LADY'S LIFE...

TO WHOM DO I HAVE THE HONOR?

BILLY FLETCHER, YOUR LORDSHIP.

I'M CHARLIE... THE FIRST!

AND THIS IS BLACK TOM OF KILBURN.

PLEASE KNOW THAT I HAVE THE GREATEST RESPECT FOR YOUR COMPATRIOTS. SEVERAL OF MY ANCESTORS HAILED FROM IRELAND...

YEAH, LOVELY... MINE, TOO.

I SAY, MISS!

DRY YOUR TEARS. YOUR FATHER IS IN GOOD HANDS, AND I SHOULD PERSONALLY LIKE TO SUPPORT HIS HEALTH EXPENSES...AND THE COSTS OF REBUILDING HIS ESTABLISHMENT...

BUT WE CAN'T ACCEPT THAT, SIR! I DON'T EVEN KNOW YOUR NAME, AND...

DO FORGIVE ME. MY NAME IS LORD NEVILLE ASPREY THE THIRD.

PLEASE MAY I OFFER MY ASSISTANCE...AND THE AID OF MY PERSONAL FORTUNE?

HE'S COMPLETELY OUT OF HIS *MIND* TO SAY THAT HERE, IN FRONT OF EV'RYONE. IT'S LIKE HE'S ASKIN' TO GET ROBBED.

THAT MIGHT DO HIM SOME GOOD...

MY FRIENDS! WHAT WOULD YOU SAY TO ACCOMPANYING ME TO MY DWELLING? YOU WILL FIND SUSTENANCE THERE, AND I WOULD BE DELIGHTED TO PROFFER YOU SOME LIQUID ASSETS IN GRATITUDE FOR YOUR SELFLESS HEROISM!

DID YA CATCH ANY O' THAT?

YEAH, I THINK HE'S INVITING US TO HIS PLACE TO EAT, AND TO GIVE US SOME CASH.

LET'S GO!

WONDERFUL! WE JUST NEED TO HAIL A CAB!

OH, FATHER! MY POOR FATHER! I SHOULD BE AT HIS SIDE...

HE'LL BE FINE! IT WAS JUST SOME SMOKE. I'M SURE HE'LL BE BACK ON HIS FEET SOON! MEANWHILE, ALLOW ME TO OFFER MY SUPPORT...

I BEG YOUR PARDON?!

I UNDERSTAND YOUR DISARRAY, MISS, BUT STILL, THIS UNFORTUNATE ACCIDENT COULD HAVE BEEN--

IT WAS NO ACCIDENT!

IS YER DAD GETTIN' SWINDLED, THEN?

YES, BY A MAN NAMED **HARRY SYKES**. HE RUNS THE WHOLE DISTRICT, AND...

NO NEED TO CARRY ON. WE GET THE PICTURE...

BUT I UNDERSTAND **NONE** OF THIS, I'M AFRAID...

SOME THUGS ARE EXTORTING MONEY FROM MISS CORBETT'S FATHER, REPUTEDLY IN EXCHANGE FOR THEIR PROTECTION. THEY BURNED DOWN THE MINSTREL BECAUSE HE COULDN'T PAY.

MY GOD! I HAD NO IDEA THAT... WHO ARE THESE AWFUL INDIVIDUALS? WE ABSOLUTELY MUST TELL THE POLICE!

NO! CERTAINLY NOT! THEY'D FIND OUT, AND THEN PERCY WOULD HURT MY FATHER...OR ME. HE...

PERCY? NOT... **BLOODY PERCY?!**

YES. Y-YOU... KNOW HIM?

IT DON'T RING A BELL.

HE'S THE **WORST** KIND OF RUFFIAN! LOOKS LIKE A LADIES' MAN, BUT HE'S BLOODTHIRSTY. HE ONCE BEAT A STRUMPET IN THE FACE WITH HIS CANE FOR LOOKING AT HIM THE WRONG WAY.

HE'S INSANE. THINKS HE'S AN ARISTOCRAT... GOES ROUND SAYING HE'S A **ROYAL BASTARD** OR SOME SUCH...

YOU'RE PRETTY WELL-INFORMED, AIN'T YA?

WHEN MY MOTHER WAS ALIVE, SHE TOLD ME TO BEWARE OF HIM. HE MUST'VE BEEN 14 OR 15 BACK THEN, BUT HE WAS ALREADY A TERROR. HE USED TO PREY ON YOUNGER GIRLS...

OURS, MY LORD... OURS...

MY GOD, WHAT KIND OF WORLD **IS** THIS?

GOD ALMIGHTY, MABEL! WHAT ARE YOU DOING HERE IN THE MIDDLE OF THE NIGHT?

OH, IT'S YOU, MR. PERKINS! YOU SCARED THE LIFE OUT OF ME!

IT'S...THE YOUNG MASTER, SIR! HE JUST GOT BACK...WITH FRIENDS, AND HE TOLD ME TO...

WHAT SORT OF FRIENDS?

AH, PERKINS. JUST IN TIME! PLEASE GET THE FIRE GOING, WOULD YOU? IT'S FREEZING IN HERE!

YES, YOUR LORDSHIP, I...

COME NOW, DON'T LOOK SO DEJECTED, OLD CHAP! ISN'T A GENTLEMAN ENTITLED TO BRING BACK A FEW IMPROMPTU GUESTS FOR A MIDNIGHT SNACK?

CHEERS, MISS! AND CAN WE HAVE A SAUCER O' MILK FOR THE CAT, AS WELL?

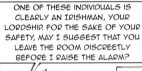

ONE OF THESE INDIVIDUALS IS CLEARLY AN IRISHMAN, YOUR LORDSHIP. FOR THE SAKE OF YOUR SAFETY, MAY I SUGGEST THAT YOU LEAVE THE ROOM DISCREETLY BEFORE I RAISE THE ALARM?

NEVILLE! WHAT THE... WHO ARE THESE...PEOPLE?

AH, MOTHER! FORGIVE ME FOR AWAKENING YOU, BUT SINCE YOU'RE HERE...

ALLOW ME TO INTRODUCE A FEW FRIENDS.

ALRIGHT, MA'AM?!

WILLIAM FLETCHER, MY LADY. SORRY FOR THE NOISE AND EVERYTHING.

DON'T MIND HER. MOTHER CAN BE RATHER THEATRICAL SOMETIMES.

WELL, IT ONLY REMAINS FOR US TO THANK YOU FOR--

YOU CAN'T LEAVE NOW! I HAVE SOME EXTREMELY IMPORTANT MATTERS TO DISCUSS WITH YOU...

REALLY?

AS I MENTIONED, I INTEND TO PROVIDE ASSISTANCE TO MISS CORBETT AND HER FATHER. BUT I WILL NEED A FEW DAYS TO...GET IT ALL READY, OF COURSE.

IN THE MEANTIME, COULD YOU KEEP AN EYE ON MISS CORBETT TO ENSURE THAT NO HARM SHOULD BEFALL HER? YOU SEEM TO BE FAMILIAR WITH THE TYPE OF INDIVIDUALS WHO...

ER, ALL DUE RESPECT, BUT WE DON'T WORK FER YA.

OBVIOUSLY THE JOB WOULD BE REMUNERATED. LET'S SEE... WOULD TWELVE GUINEAS BE A SUFFICIENT SALARY?

TWELVE GUINEAS? BUT THAT'S... THAT'S...

THAT'S PERFECT!

YOU CAN COUNT ON US, YOUR LORDSHIP! WE ALREADY HAVE CERTAIN EXPERIENCE IN SUCH JOBS.

YOU'RE TELLING ME! WITH THE OTHER DOZEN GUINEAS HE ADDED FOR SAVING HIS SKIN, IT AMOUNTS TO...ER, A FORTUNE! WE CAN BUY NEW SHOES AND...LOTS OF OTHER STUFF!

WELL, YA GOTTA ADMIT ONE THING: HE AIN'T STINGY!

DON'T WORRY, I'M SURE IT'LL ALL WORK OUT FOR YOU AND YER DAD...

YEAH! IT'S OUR TURN TO DRESS UP LIKE LORDS!

I WISH I COULD BELIEVE IT...

I DON'T DOUBT THAT LORD NEVILLE'S INTENTIONS ARE SINCERE, BUT HIS FAMILY WILL NEVER LET HIM...RUIN THEIR REPUTATION WITH...

LISTEN, THERE'S SOMETHIN' WE DIDN'T TELL YA: WE'RE WORKIN' FOR SHERLOCK HOLMES.

SHERLOCK HOLMES?

LORD NEVILLE ASPREY?

THE THIRD... WHEN HE STARTED ACTING ALL PRINCELY IN THE MIDDLE OF THE STREET, SCABS AND SCRUFFY WERE WITHIN EARSHOT, OF COURSE.

THEY IMMEDIATELY THOUGHT THE TIP MIGHT INTEREST ME... I MEAN US, HARRY.

AND WHY IS THAT?

I KNOW A THING OR TWO ABOUT THE ASPREYS. THEY'RE STINKING RICH AND DON'T KNOW WHAT TO DO WITH IT ALL. BUT THAT CRETIN DOESN'T HAVE AN OUNCE OF COMMON SENSE. HE'D BE EASY TO TRAP.

WE CAN MAKE HIM BELIEVE WE HAVE CORBETT'S DAUGHTER. HE'LL RUSH IN LIKE PRINCE CHARMING, AND WE'LL GRAB HIM AND HOLD HIM TO RANSOM.

I KNOW HOW RICH FOLK BEHAVE, HARRY...

HIS FAMILY WILL DO ANYTHING TO SAVE ITS HEIR... AND AVOID A SCANDAL. TRUST ME, THEY WON'T BE AFRAID TO COUGH UP THEIR CASH!

SO WHAT DO YOU SAY?

I SAY IT'S TOO RISKY, PERCY. THIS IS A BUSINESS, YOU UNDERSTAND? COMMERCE! KIDNAPPIN' LORDS AIN'T OUR DEPARTMENT.

BUT IT'S A GOLDEN OPPORTUNITY, HARRY! LET ME HANDLE IT WITH A FEW OF MY BOYS, AND IF IT WORKS OUT...

I SAID NO! LEAVE THE TOFFS ALONE, CLEAR?

ALL CLEAR, HARRY. YOU'RE THE BOSS.

RIGHT. AND IF YOU'VE GOT A PROBLEM WITH IT, YA CAN GO BACK TO PLAYIN' THE DANDY IN THE GUTTER WHERE I FOUND YA!

HELLO, UNCLE. I WAS JUST INTENDING TO SPEAK TO YOU ABOUT--

NO, MY BOY! IT IS I WHO SHALL SPEAK AND YOU WHO SHALL LISTEN!

I SAY, UNCLE, IT SEEMS YOU'VE FORGOTTEN WHOM YOU'RE ADDRESSING. I AM LORD NEV--

SILENCE!

THE TITLE YOU HAVE INHERITED DOESN'T CHANGE WHAT YOU ARE: A SPOILED LITTLE BRAT WHO CAN'T TELL WHIMS FROM REALITY! YOUR POOR MOTHER INFORMED ME OF YOUR GROTESQUE PLANS...

...AND OF THE VISITORS YOU DARED TO BRING BACK HERE, TO HER HOME! DO YOU THINK FOR ONE INSTANT THAT I WILL ALLOW YOU TO FRITTER THE FAMILY FORTUNE?

BUT IT'S NOTHING OF THE SORT. I SIMPLY...

AND THE 24 GUINEAS YOU GAVE THOSE LOUSY BEGGARS? I KNOW EVERYTHING, YOU SEE!

24 GUINEAS? IT'S NOTHING TO US, BUT A FORTUNE TO THEM!

INDEED, YOU YOUNG DOLT! BUT IF PEOPLE LEARN THAT YOU'RE HANDING OUT GUINEAS TO ALL AND SUNDRY, EVERY GUTTERSNIPE IN THE EAST END WILL SOON BESIEGE US!

THOSE "GUTTERSNIPES" SAVED MY LIFE, UNCLE! DAMN IT, SUCH A FUSS OVER 24 GUINEAS? I DIDN'T KNOW THAT GREED WAS ONE OF YOUR VICES!

FLAC

NOW THAT YOU HAVE SHUT YOUR TRAP, LISTEN VERY CAREFULLY, YOU WHELP! YOU ARE STILL A MINOR, AND AS LONG AS I HEAD THE FAMILY COUNCIL, WHAT YOU CALL "YOUR FORTUNE" STAYS UNDER MY CONTROL!

FOR THE LAST TIME, NEVILLE: GIVE UP THAT GIRL AND ALL YOUR ESCAPADES IMMEDIATELY...OR YOU WILL FACE THE CONSEQUENCES OF YOUR ACTIONS!

HAVEN'T I SIMPLY BEHAVED AS A *GENTLEMAN* OUGHT TO BEHAVE? AH, BUT SILLY ME! YOU DON'T EVEN KNOW THE *MEANING* OF THE WORD...

IT'S OVER, MY BOY! AND, BELIEVE ME, YOU WILL REGRET THIS.

SHHH, WATSON... KEEP STILL OR THEY'LL BOOT US OUT.

EXCUSE ME, MISS. I'M OSCAR CORBETT'S DAUGHTER. THEY TOLD ME HIS ROOM IS...

CORBETT? HE'S IN THE WARD DOWN THERE...

24 GUINEAS! I CAN'T BELIEVE IT! THAT'S...ER...EIGHT GUINEAS EACH. CAN YOU IMAGINE?

YEAH... IT'S A HELLUVA LOT...

WE NEEDN'T TELL MISTER HOLMES ABOUT IT. IF HE KNOWS WE'RE FILTHY RICH, HE'LL STOP GIVIN' US JOBS...

SO WHAT? FORGET HIM! WE'RE FREE AGENTS NOW! LIFE IS SWEET!

YOU REALLY ARE A RASCAL...

YUP, AND PROUD OF IT! SPEAKIN' O' WHICH, I'VE GOT AN UNBEATABLE TRICK FER WINNIN' ON THE HORSES, SO LONG AS THE STAKES ARE HIGH ENOUGH. IF YA'D CARE TO INVEST...

NO, THANK YOU. AND YOU, CHARLIE? WHAT WILL YOU DO WITH IT?

I DON'T REALLY KNOW...

YA SHOULD PUT A PROPER WEDDIN' TROUSSEAU TOGETHER, IF YA EVER WANNA FIND A...

OUCH!

SORRY, IT DID IT ALL BY ITSELF...

SO, WHAT'S YER TRICK FOR THE GEE-GEES, THEN?

FATHER!

WELL, HELLO, GRACE...

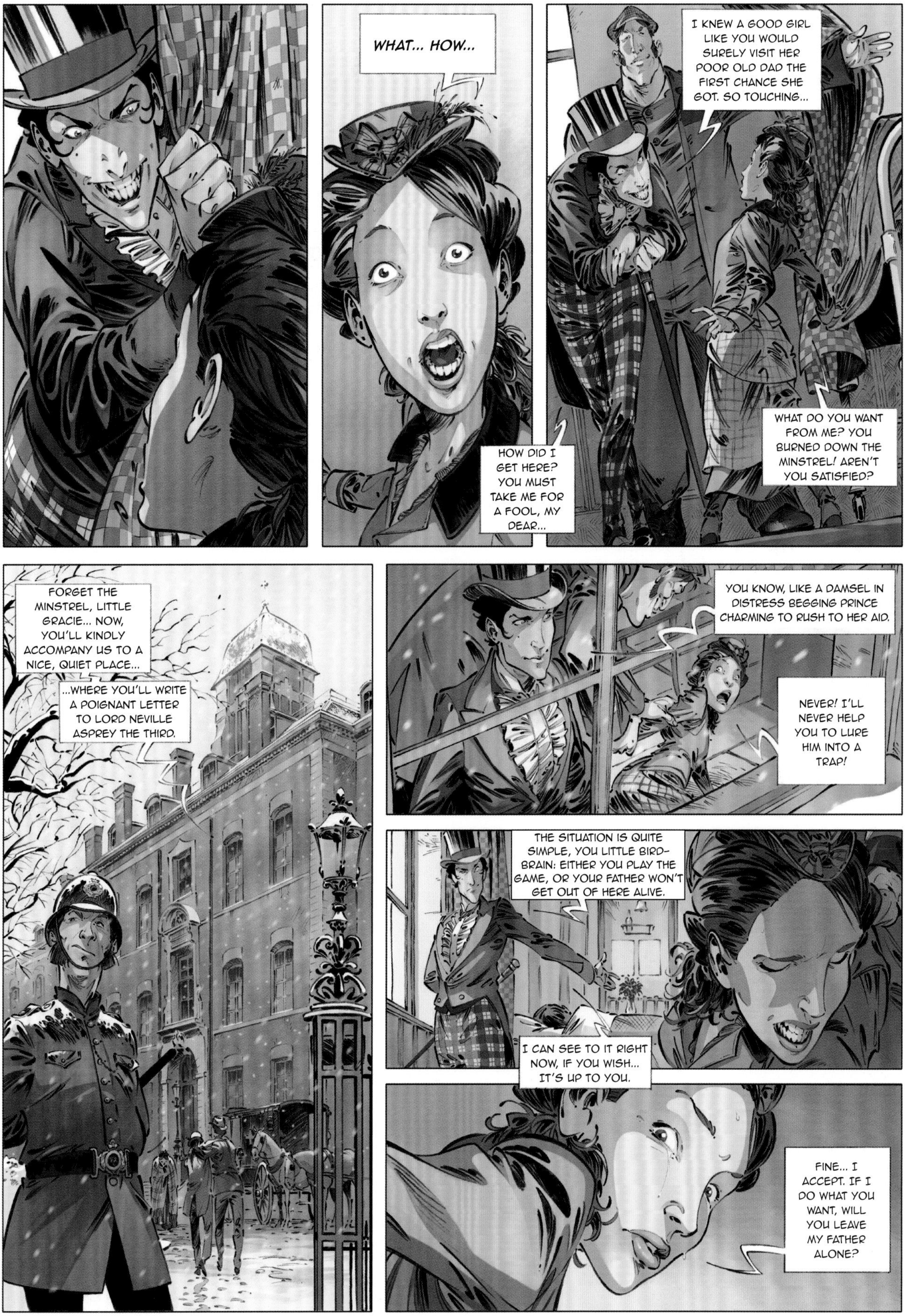
WHAT... HOW...
HOW DID I GET HERE? YOU MUST TAKE ME FOR A FOOL, MY DEAR...
I KNEW A GOOD GIRL LIKE YOU WOULD SURELY VISIT HER POOR OLD DAD THE FIRST CHANCE SHE GOT. SO TOUCHING...
WHAT DO YOU WANT FROM ME? YOU BURNED DOWN THE MINSTREL! AREN'T YOU SATISFIED?
FORGET THE MINSTREL, LITTLE GRACIE... NOW, YOU'LL KINDLY ACCOMPANY US TO A NICE, QUIET PLACE...
...WHERE YOU'LL WRITE A POIGNANT LETTER TO LORD NEVILLE ASPREY THE THIRD.
YOU KNOW, LIKE A DAMSEL IN DISTRESS BEGGING PRINCE CHARMING TO RUSH TO HER AID.
NEVER! I'LL NEVER HELP YOU TO LURE HIM INTO A TRAP!
THE SITUATION IS QUITE SIMPLE, YOU LITTLE BIRD-BRAIN: EITHER YOU PLAY THE GAME, OR YOUR FATHER WON'T GET OUT OF HERE ALIVE.
I CAN SEE TO IT RIGHT NOW, IF YOU WISH... IT'S UP TO YOU.
FINE... I ACCEPT. IF I DO WHAT YOU WANT, WILL YOU LEAVE MY FATHER ALONE?

PERHAPS I **SHOULD** BRANCH OUT ON MY OWN? AFTER ALL, MR. HOLMES TAKES ALL THE REALLY IMPORTANT AND WEIRD CASES...

...BUT THERE ARE ALSO LOTS OF FOLKS WITH MORE ORDINARY PROBLEMS WHO MIGHT BE IN NEED OF A DETEC--

OI, LOOK! WHO ARE THEM TWO BLOKES WITH GRACE?

THE DANDY... IT'S...

IT'S BLOODY PERCY! HE'S...

THEY'RE MAKIN' FER THE STAIRS! HURRY UP!

STOP! STOP THOSE MEN! IT'S A KIDNAPPING!

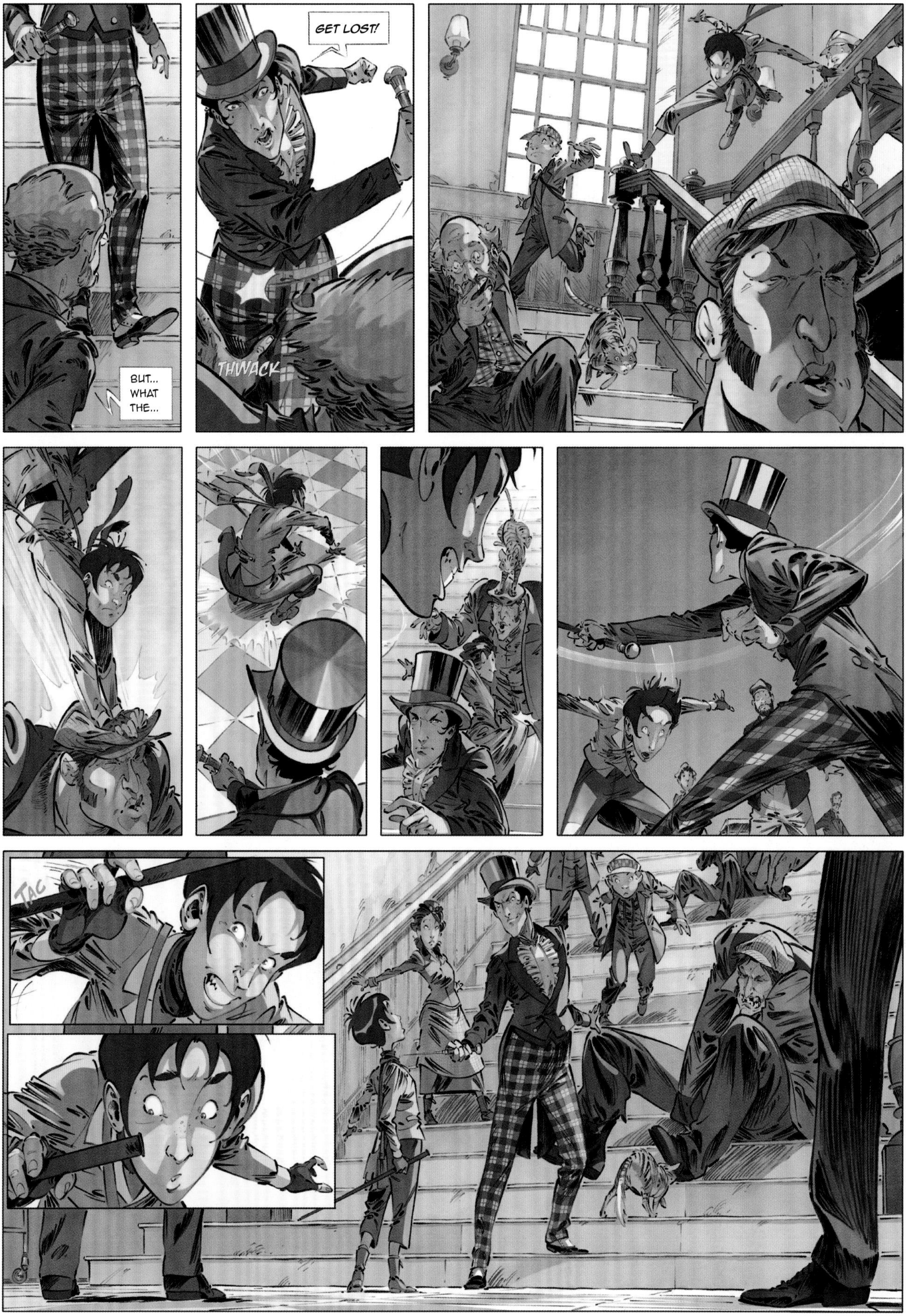
BUT... WHAT THE...
GET LOST!
THWACK
TAC

TOM!

POLICE! CALL THE POLICE!

THE SWINE STABBED HIM!

TOM! BUT...

IT'S ALRIGHT, HE MISSED!

QUICK! THEY'RE RUNNIN' TO THE PARK!

PERHAPS WE SHOULD...

NO TIME!

LET ME GO, YOU BULLIES!

SHUT UP!

HURRY!

THOSE BRATS ARE HOT ON OUR HEELS! MUST LOSE THEM BEFORE THEY BRING THE COPPERS!

THIS WAY!

29

WATSON!

CRAACK

KRAAACCC

DAMN IT...

PERCY! HELP ME, FOR GOD'S SAKE!

CORNERED LIKE A RAT, BLOODY PERCY! THE POLICE WILL BE ALONG ANY MINUTE! GIVE UP WITHOUT A FIGHT, YOU SWINE!

HANDS OFF, IDIOT!

SHTACK

WE WILL MEET AGAIN! THIS IS *NOT* OVER!

AND YOU, *BLACKHEAD*... I'M GOING TO KILL YOU!

BLIMEY, WE WERE IN HOT WATER THERE... SO TO SPEAK!

GOOD ON YA, TOM! YOU WERE BRILLIANT!

MRROW

A POLICEMAN! NO... IF THEY GET INVOLVED... MY FATHER...

WE'D PROB'LY BEST CLEAR OFF BEFORE ANY MORE OF 'EM SHOW UP!

COME ON!

WHERE... ARE WE GOING?

WHERE WE SHOULD HAVE GONE A LONG TIME AGO... CONSIDERING THE WAY THINGS HAVE TURNED OUT, I THINK IT'S HIGH TIME WE INFORMED MR. HOLMES...

OH YEAH? WHAT FOR? IF IT'S TO FIND OUT WHO'S GUILTY, I'LL REMIND YA THAT WE ALREADY KNOW, BILLY BOY...

BILLY'S RIGHT, TOM. WE CAN'T LEAVE HOLMES OUTTA THIS ONE. BESIDES, IT'S PARTLY HIS FAULT THAT WE'RE IN THIS MESS, INNIT?

THAT'S FER SURE!

I RECKON HE SHOULD HELP US SORT IT OUT, DON'T YOU?

GUESS SO...

AND GRACE LOOKS LIKE SHE NEEDS A NICE CUP O' TEA... AND A FEW SCONES, MAYBE.

I'M SURE THAT MRS. HUDSON CAN...

ALRIGHT, ALRIGHT! YA WIN! LET'S GO.

JUST LOOK AT TOM BACK THERE... LORD NEVILLE MIGHT BE GETTIN' A RIVAL...

TOM'S ALWAYS BEEN PARTIAL TO GIRLS WITH PRETTY VOICES. MUST BE HIS IRISH ORIGINS. THE CELTIC SOUL, AND ALL THAT...

IT'S ALWAYS THE SAME! WHENEVER YA NEED HIM, HE AIN'T THERE!

MR. HOLMES RETURNED LAST NIGHT BUT JUST LEFT AGAIN WITHOUT TELLING ME WHEN HE'D BE BACK. AN URGENT CASE, HE SAID...

HOW DO YOU MEAN, HE ISN'T HOME?

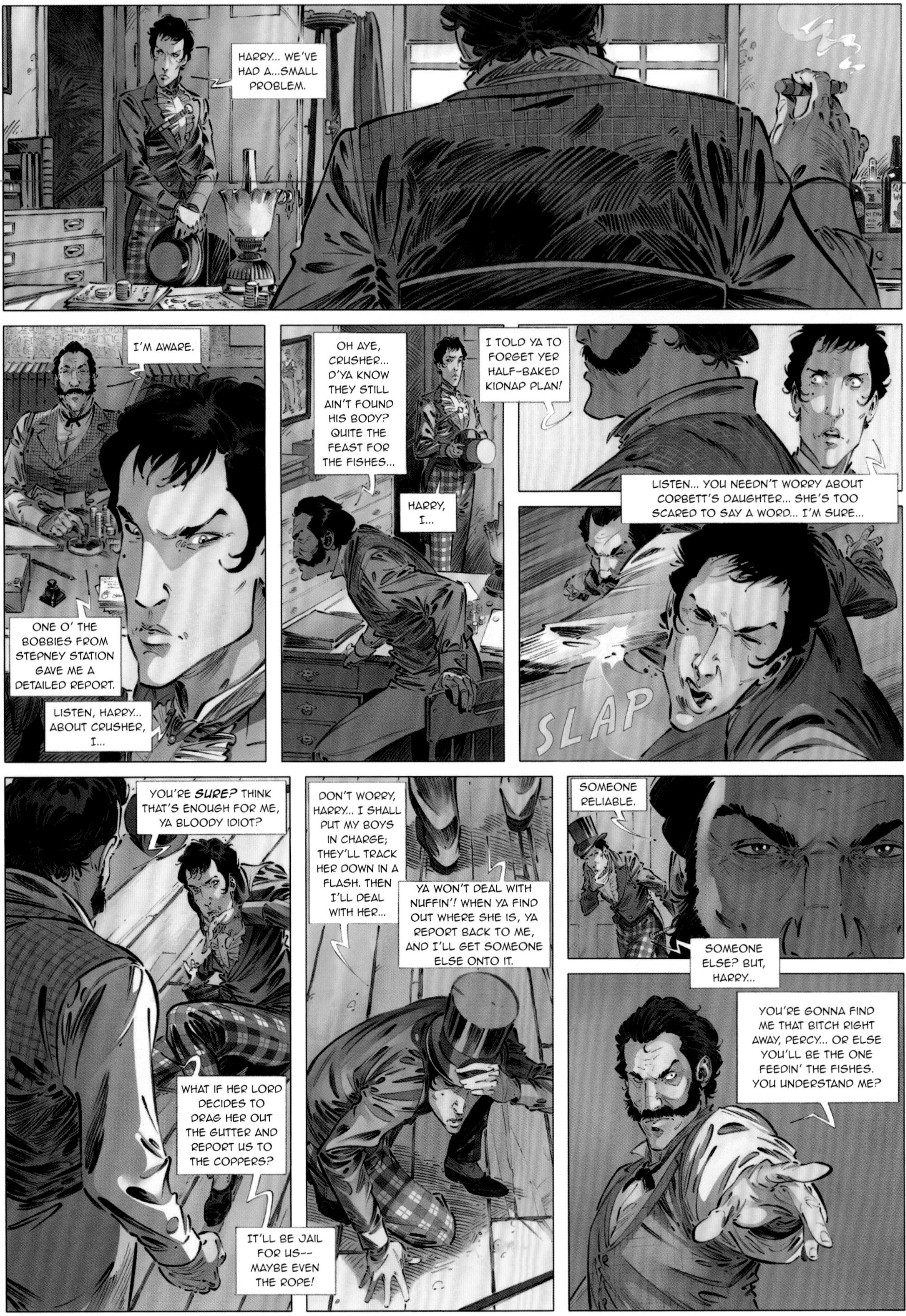
HARRY... WE'VE HAD A...SMALL PROBLEM.
I'M AWARE.
ONE O' THE BOBBIES FROM STEPNEY STATION GAVE ME A DETAILED REPORT.
LISTEN, HARRY... ABOUT CRUSHER, I...
OH AYE, CRUSHER... D'YA KNOW THEY STILL AIN'T FOUND HIS BODY? QUITE THE FEAST FOR THE FISHES...
HARRY, I...
I TOLD YA TO FORGET YER HALF-BAKED KIDNAP PLAN!
LISTEN... YOU NEEDN'T WORRY ABOUT CORBETT'S DAUGHTER... SHE'S TOO SCARED TO SAY A WORD... I'M SURE...
SLAP
YOU'RE SURE? THINK THAT'S ENOUGH FOR ME, YA BLOODY IDIOT?
WHAT IF HER LORD DECIDES TO DRAG HER OUT THE GUTTER AND REPORT US TO THE COPPERS?
IT'LL BE JAIL FOR US-- MAYBE EVEN THE ROPE!
DON'T WORRY, HARRY... I SHALL PUT MY BOYS IN CHARGE; THEY'LL TRACK HER DOWN IN A FLASH. THEN I'LL DEAL WITH HER...
YA WON'T DEAL WITH NUFFIN'! WHEN YA FIND OUT WHERE SHE IS, YA REPORT BACK TO ME, AND I'LL GET SOMEONE ELSE ONTO IT.
SOMEONE RELIABLE.
SOMEONE ELSE? BUT, HARRY...
YOU'RE GONNA FIND ME THAT BITCH RIGHT AWAY, PERCY... OR ELSE YOU'LL BE THE ONE FEEDIN' THE FISHES. YOU UNDERSTAND ME?

KEEP THE CHANGE, MY GOOD MAN!

I ABSOLUTELY MUST SPEAK TO LORD NEVILLE. I KNOW HIS FEELINGS ARE SINCERE, BUT HIS FAMILY... THEY'LL NEVER ACCEPT US. IT WAS SENSELESS FROM THE START.

THESE RICH FOLKS AIN'T GONNA BE HAPPY TO SEE US AGAIN!

A MAN OF HIS STATION... IT JUST WASN'T MEANT TO BE. BUT I MUST SPEAK TO HIM AGAIN ONE LAST TIME, TO EXPLAIN THINGS...

PITY, IT'D HAVE BEEN SO ROMANTIC...

SHE'S RIGHT, BILLY! THEY'RE FROM DIFFERENT WORLDS, THAT'S ALL...

ER... GOOD DAY... IS LORD NEV...

HIS LORDSHIP NO LONGER WISHES TO SEE YOU.

PLEASE REFRAIN FROM ANY FURTHER...ATTEMPTS TO BREAK IN, OR YOU'LL BE DEALING WITH THE POLICE.

BUT I ONLY WANTED TO--

VLAM

WELL, AT LEAST THAT PART'S CLEAR...

HE...DIDN'T EVEN COME TO TALK TO ME...

YES, IT IS RATHER ODD... PERHAPS THEY'RE KEEPING HIM LOCKED UP? UPPER-CLASS FAMILIES SOMETIMES DO THAT, APPARENTLY...

THAT'S IT, THE DETECTIVE KING IS OFF AGAIN.

35

NOW, YOU LISTEN HERE...

WOULD YOU REALLY DO THAT FOR ME, TOM?

WHAT IF YA WANDER ROUND TO THE BACK DOOR, TOM? P'RAPS THEIR LI'L MAID COULD TELL YA MORE? I RECKON SHE TOOK A FANCY TO YA THE OTHER NIGHT... CELTIC CHARM, AND ALL THAT...

SHE SAYS SOME MEN IN BLACK CAME TO GET NEVILLE THIS MORNIN' AND TOOK HIM AWAY IN A CAB.

HE TRIED TO FIGHT, BUT THREE OF 'EM BUNDLED HIM OFF.

WHAT, AND NOBODY FROM THE HOUSE INTERVENED?

SYKES! I'M POSITIVE THAT SYKES IS BEHIND ALL THIS!

I DON'T THINK SO, GRACE. THEM FELLAS... IT'S NEVILLE'S UNCLE--SIR CHARLES WHATSISNAME-- WHO CALLED 'EM.

LORD NEVILLE'S UNCLE IN LEAGUE WITH SYKES'S GANG? THIS CASE IS GETTING DAMN COMPLICATED! WE MUST TELL MISTER HOLMES!

DON'T BOTHER, BILLY... THEM FELLAS WERE NOTHIN' TA DO WITH SYKES.

JENNY THE MAID OPENED THE DOOR TO 'EM. SIR CHARLES WAS EXPECTIN' ONE OF 'EM... SHE CAN'T REMEMBER HIS NAME, BUT SHE SAID HE LOOKED LIKE AN UNDERTAKER...

BIG GEEZER, FACE A FOOT LONG, DARK HAIR, AND BUSHY BLACK EYEBROWS?

THAT'S RIGHT! HOW DID YA...?

THE LUNATIC ASYLUM? BUT... HOW COULD HIS UNCLE AND HIS OWN MOTHER... WHY?

I KNOW WHO HE IS. HIS NAME'S *SIMS*. HE'S IN CHARGE O' BEDLAM...

PROBABLY BECAUSE HE REFUSED TO "SEE SENSE" ABOUT THE TWO OF YOU...

THAT'S DISGUSTIN'...

IT'S TERRIBLE!

HOW COULD THEY?

HIS OWN MOTHER...

WE HAVE TO DO SOMETHING!

WE CAN'T LEAVE HIM TO ROT IN THERE! IT'S MONSTROUS!

I'VE GOT TO SEE HIM!

WE'RE ALL GOIN'!

ACTUALLY, BEDLAM AIN'T AS AWFUL AS YA THINK. I KNOW IT WELL. I SOMETIMES GO TO VISIT ME MUM. SHE'S IN THERE TOO...

BUT FOR GENTLEMEN AND ALL, THEY'VE GOT THESE CELL-- ER, SPECIAL APARTMENTS...

A LORD LIKE HIM... THEY WOULDN'T DARE STICK HIM IN WITH... ALL THE REST. IT'LL BE LIKE A HOTEL FOR HIM, ALMOST...

REALLY?

BUT LAST TIME WE TALKED ABOUT IT, YOU SAID THAT IT WAS HELL IN THERE!

A REAL NIGHTM--

OOPS...

WELL DONE, BILLY FLETCHER...

37

SHE MUST BE OUT OF THE DISTRICT, BUT SHE CAN'T HAVE GONE FAR.

ROUND UP ALL OF YOUR CONTACTS: TRAMPS, COACHMEN, HARLOTS...

AND FLUSH HER OUT BEFORE NIGHTFALL, UNDERSTOOD?

BY THE WAY, SHE HAD THREE KIDS WITH HER...

ONE'S BLOND, ONE A BLACK-HAIRED IRISHMAN, AND THERE'S A THIRD WITH A FILTHY CAT...

FIND THEM FOR ME, TOO!

SAY, PERCY... THE IRISH KID AND THEM OTHERS WITH THE CAT... I FINK THEY WAS AT THE MINSTREL LAST NIGHT...

OH YEAH, THEY WAS WITH THAT LORD AND ALL...

I RECKON I KNOWS 'EM. IT'S BILLY FLETCHER'S GANG. THE IRISH LAD'S BLACK TOM O' KILBURN, AND THE THIRD ONE WITH THE TOMCAT... CAN'T REMEMBER HIS NAME...

AND WHAT DO YOU KNOW ABOUT THEM?

WELL... SOME SAY THEY WORKS FOR *SHERLOCK HOLMES*...

38

HELLO THERE, KID! COME TO SEE YER LOONY MOTHER, HAVE YA?

YEAH, AND I BROUGHT ME MATES ALONG...

TRIPLE THE PRICE, THEN...

RIGHT, FROM NOW ON, STICK TO ME LIKE LEECHES...

CHARLOTTE?

NOT TODAY, MUM. I'M ON A MISSION...

SO WHAT DO WE DO NOW, CHARLIE?

WE FIND *SAMMY THE SNARK*. HE KNOWS ALL WHAT GOES ON IN HERE...

SAMMY THE SNARK? I ASSUME HE'S NOT ONE OF THE STAFF...

RIGHT. SAMMY'S A BIT WEIRD, YOU'LL SEE, BUT HE'S A FINE BLOKE. JUST LEMME DO THE TALKIN' AND DON'T ASK NO QUESTIONS, ALRIGHT?

HELLO, SAMMY! HOW'S IT GOIN'?

OH, SHOEGAIN, CHARLIE! YOU'RE HERE TO GLEE YOUR SOUTHER, I JUXTAPOSE?

NAH, NOT TODAY. IT'S YOU I'M AFTER, ACTUALLY... I NEED SOME INFORMATION.

ON WHAT BISMUTH?

WELL, SAMMY, I HEARD THEY BROUGHT IN A NEW LUNA-- A NEW RESIDENT THIS MORNIN'. A YOUNG GENT, VERY REFINED...

DEFUREDLY! 'TWAS THE GRAND FEMURS SIMS HIMSELF WHO MOLED HIM IN...

POOR BLOVE, HE LOOKED GATEFULLY KLANK. IT'S RIGHT GRISMAL IN HERE, I DO ADMIT...

YOU SAID IT! GOT ANY IDEA WHERE WE CAN FIND THIS LORD, THEN?

THAT'S IT, THEN... HE'S DOWNSTAIRS. WE CAN'T GET IN--NO ONE'S ALLOWED TO VISIT THE DUNGEON...

THE DUNGEON? WHAT IS THIS, THE TOWER O' LONDON?

SINCE HE WAS GRUTTLING OVERLY, SIMS WORPED HIM DOWN WITH THE JABBERWOCKS...

IT'S DREADFUL! WE MUST DO SOMETHING! HE'LL GO MAD IN HERE!

AT THIS STAGE, I ONLY KNOW ONE PERSON WHO COULD HELP US...

AND THAT'S THE WHOLE STORY, DOCTOR... A MURKY AFFAIR WHERE GREED GOES HAND IN HAND WITH... ER...

THAT'S ENOUGH. DON'T OVERDO IT.

WHAT AN APPALLING STORY! HOW HORRIBLY UNJUST!

JOHN, YOU CAN DO SOMETHING, CAN'T YOU?

WELL, ER... I MIGHT BE ABLE TO VISIT LORD NEVILLE, BUT...

JOHN?

MISS CORBETT, I...

I SHALL VISIT BEDLAM TOMORROW MORNING.

MEANWHILE, YOU MAY STAY AT OUR HOUSE...

AND, ER... THE SAME APPLIES TO OUR YOUNG FRIENDS, OF COURSE.

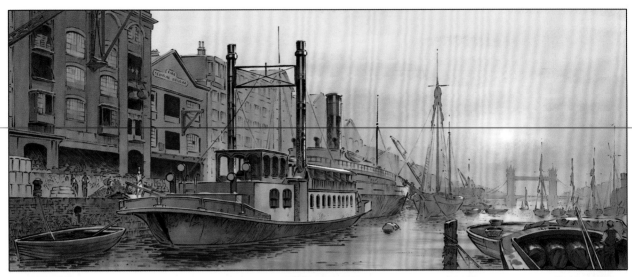

YOU WANTED A WORD, HARRY?

YEAH. LEMME INTRODUCE *JASPER CRANE*. HE'S GONNA HELP US SETTLE OUR PROBLEM.

JASPER LEARNED THE TRADE IN MANCHESTER, WORKIN' WITH FREDDIE THE PINCERS AND THE MADDOX BROTHERS. HE'S A REAL *PROFESSIONAL*... KNOW WHAT I MEAN?

HARRY, I HAVE NEWS ABOUT CORBETT'S DAUGHTER. SHE WAS SEEN TAKING A CARRIAGE RIGHT AFTER...THE PARK INCIDENT. SCABS AND HIS BOYS ARE ON THE CASE.

AND SO ARE THE COPPERS, BELIEVE IT OR NOT! NOT THE LOCALS, MIND... SEEMS A BLOKE FROM THE YARD GOT WIND O' YER LI'L SHOW AT THE HOSPITAL AND THE PARK... LESTRADE--NAME RING ANY BELLS?

I RAN INTO HIM BACK WHEN I WAS A COPPER... HE'S THE SNOOPIN' TYPE. CAN'T BE BOUGHT.

JASPER, AS SOON AS PERCY FINDS THAT BITCH, YOU DEAL WITH HER.

RIGHT Y'ARE. AND THE FATHER?

AS LONG AS HIS DARLIN' DAUGHTER IS AT LARGE, CORBETT'LL KEEP QUIET.

HE'LL BELIEVE WE'VE GOT HER. WE CAN DEAL WITH HIM LATER.

SHE'S OUR PRIORITY.

I'M NOT SURE I FULLY UNDERSTAND THE *REASON* FOR YOUR VISIT, DR....WATSON, WAS IT?

AS I TOLD YOU, I HAVE BEEN APPOINTED BY A PERSON WHO WISHES TO REMAIN ANONYMOUS TO ASCERTAIN WHETHER LORD NEVILLE ASPREY HAS BEEN IMPROPERLY CONFINED IN YOUR ESTABLISHMENT.

MAY I SEE THE MEDICAL CERTIFICATE THAT CONFIRMS HIS INSANITY?

LORD NEVILLE WILL BE EXAMINED BY OUR DOCTORS AS SOON AS POSSIBLE.

I SEE. SO HE DEFINITELY *HAS* BEEN CONFINED ARBITRARILY...

CERTAINLY NOT. LORD NEVILLE'S FAMILY...

I IMAGINE YOU MEAN HIS UNCLE, SIR CHARLES ASPREY, WHO JUST SO HAPPENS TO BE ONE OF YOUR INSTITUTION'S MAIN BENEFACTORS?

INDEED.

SINCE YOU ARE SO WELL-INFORMED, YOU SHOULD THINK TWICE BEFORE MEDDLING IN THE AFFAIRS OF SUCH AN INFLUENTIAL FIGURE AS SIR CHARLES. I DOUBT HE WOULD APPRECIATE--

WELL, I CAN SEE I AM WASTING MY TIME. I SHALL RETURN IN A FEW DAYS WITH MY FRIEND *SHERLOCK HOLMES.*

SHERLOCK HOLMES? OH... YOU... YOU'RE *THAT* WATSON?

WHAT WOULD YOU SAY TO *A SCANDAL IN BEDLAM* AS A TITLE? QUITE CATCHY, DON'T YOU THINK?

YES, THE VERY SAME. NATURALLY, IF MR. HOLMES WERE TO VISIT YOUR ESTABLISHMENT, I WOULD BE OBLIGED, AS HIS BIOGRAPHER, TO CHRONICLE THE INVESTIGATION...

WHAT DO YOU TAKE ME FOR? MY FAMILY HAS RUN THIS INSTITUTION SINCE THE DAYS OF KING GEORGE! DO YOU REALLY THINK YOU CAN INTIMIDATE ME? *YOU WILL LEAVE THIS BUILDING IMMEDIATELY!*

IF YOU THINK I WILL LEAVE IT AT THAT, YOU ARE SORELY MISTAKEN!

THE CHOICE IS YOURS, DOCTOR...

ASSAIL MY REPUTATION AND I WILL TARNISH YOURS! YOU'LL LOSE ALL YOUR CLIENTS AND BE BARRED FROM THE MEDICAL PROFESSION!

BUT YOU'LL STILL HAVE YOUR PENNY DREADFULS TO FALL BACK ON...

NELSON&Co
PRINTING
OFFICES.

WELL?

WELL DONE, SCABS. I KNEW I COULD COUNT ON YOU...

THEY FOUND THE GIRL. THESE KIDS ARE REAL PROS. I'LL DEAL WITH HER TONIGHT; IT WON'T TAKE LONG.

NO, YA WON'T. I'M TO HANDLE IT. MR. SYKES WERE VERY CLEAR ABOUT THAT. SO, D'YA TRUST THIS TIP?

SCABS AND HIS MATES KNOW EVERY COACHMAN IN THE DAMN CITY--THEY'RE REAL PROS, I TELL YOU. ANYHOW, THE NEWS IS THAT THE GIRL AND THE THREE BRATS WERE DROPPED OFF AT A BOURGEOIS KENSINGTON ADDRESS...

PROBABLY SOME GOOD-SAMARITAN TYPES WHO EASE THEIR CONSCIENCES BY HELPING PAUPERS... THE SCUM! THEY'RE GOING TO REGRET THEIR CHARITY--SO SAYS BLOODY PERCY!

KNOCK IT OFF, WILL YA?

THESE BISCUITS ARE AWFULLY GOOD, MRS. WATSON.

YOUR FOUR-LEGGED COMPANION HAS A HEARTY APPETITE! WHAT'S HIS NAME?

ER... IT'S...

HE AIN'T REALLY GOT ONE...

AH, I THINK I RECOGNIZE JOHN'S FOOTSTEPS...

I FAILED. I AM SORRY.

JOHN?

THAT SIMS IS AS DEVIOUS AS HE IS OBSTINATE... IF ONLY HOLMES WERE WITH US...

DON'T TAKE IT TO HEART, DOCTOR. YOU DID ALL YOU COULD.

I AM SURE LORD NEVILLE HASN'T EVEN BEEN EXAMINED BY A DOCTOR. BUT NOW SIMS WILL RUSH TO HAVE AN UNSCRUPULOUS COLLEAGUE FABRICATE A CERTIFICATE OF INSANITY...

IN SHORT, WE AIN'T GOT MUCH TIME. DON'T WORRY, DOC, WE'LL DO THIS OUR WAY.

CHARLIE--YOU DRAW A MAP O' THE BLOODY MADHOUSE. BILLY--YOU FIND A GRAPPLIN' HOOK AND ABOUT 30 FEET O' ROPE. YA CAN PAY FER IT OUTTA MY SHARE...

AND I'M OFF TO LOOK THE PLACE OVER...

MRS. WATSON, COULD YA TAKE CARE O' GRACE AT YER PLACE AGAIN TONIGHT WHILE WE BREAK HIS LORDSHIP OUT?

ARE YOU... JOKING?

BLACK TOM AIN'T REALLY GOT A SENSE OF HUMOR, DOCTOR.

BUT...YOU'RE TALKING ABOUT BREAKING THE LAW!

COME ON, DOCTOR, YOU'VE BEEN HOUSEBREAKING WITH MR. HOLMES...AND MORE THAN ONCE, EH?

BUT THAT'S DIFFERENT! EVERY TIME I HELPED HOLMES WITH...THAT TYPE OF EXPEDITION, IT WAS... IT WAS...

FOR A GOOD CAUSE?

VERY WELL. HOW CAN I HELP YOU?

THEY'RE PRETTY WORKED UP TONIGHT...

SHUT UP, YA BUNCH O' LOONIES!

CLANG

MUST BE THE FULL MOON.

MAKES 'EM EVEN MADDER THAN USUAL...

RIGHT, YOU LEAD US FROM NOW ON...

GOOD GOD! IT'S LIKE WE'RE IN THE LAIR OF MR. HYDE...OR VARNEY THE VAMPIRE, OR SWEENEY TODD THE DEMON BARBER, OR...

SHUT UP!

FINE... WELL, I'LL BE ON LOOKOUT BY THE STAIRS. I'LL WARN YOU IF...

NO BLABBERIN'! YOU'RE BOTH GONNA HELP ME! I DON'T WANNA BE HERE ALL NIGHT!

KEEP CALM-- 'SPECIALLY IF ANY OF 'EM START SCREAMIN'...

NO NEWSPAPERS FOR ME TODAY, THANK YOU.

I FOUND HIM!

BILLY? BUT HOW...

SHH, YOUR LORDSHIP! WE'RE GETTING YOU OUT OF HERE.

DO YOU HAVE THE KEY?

NO, BUT BLACK TOM'S A BURG-- A FIRST-CLASS LOCKSMITH. HE'LL PICK IT IN TEN SECONDS!

THERE... THE SECOND FLOOR.

THERE'S LIGHT IN THE WINDOW...

HIDE!

THAT'S HER, THE GIRL! WHAT SHALL WE DO?

SHALL WE WAIT TILL SHE'S IN BED OR BUMP HER OFF RIGHT NOW?

I'M HANDLIN' THIS JOB. ORDERS FROM MR. SYKES.

YOU STAY OUTSIDE AND KEEP WATCH. AND NO MESSIN' AROUND!

HOW MUCH LONGER? THOUGHT YOU WERE A VIRTUOSO LOCKSMITH...

SHUT UP! YOU'RE BREAKIN' MY CONSHENTRATION! THAT'SH IT, I'M CLOSHE, I...

HURRY UP! I THINK I HEARD A NOISE...

CLAC

BUT... HOW DID...

WE CAN CHAT LATER! NOW WE NEED TO SCARPER!

ALL RIGHT THEN, LET'S "SCARPER"...

!!!

SOUND THE ALARM!

LORD NEVILLE ASPREY, I PRESUME? MY NAME IS JOHN WATSON...

NATURALLY, I SUPPOSE YOUR... SWIFT DEPARTURE FROM BEDLAM WILL CAUSE QUITE A STIR...

NOT TO WORRY, DOCTOR. FAMILIES SUCH AS MINE LOATHE SCANDALS! YOU CAN COUNT ON MY UNCLE—AND THE SINISTER SIMS—TO QUICKLY HUSH UP THIS SORDID AFFAIR...

I CAN'T WAIT TO HAVE A FRANK TALK WITH SIR CHARLES, MAN TO MAN... BUT, ABOVE ALL, I'M LONGING TO MEET MISS CORBETT AGAIN! GRACE...

SHE EAGERLY AWAITS YOUR RETURN, YOUR LORDSHIP. AND I MUST SAY—

"HERE WE ARE!"

OI! LOOK THERE!

BLOODY PERCY!

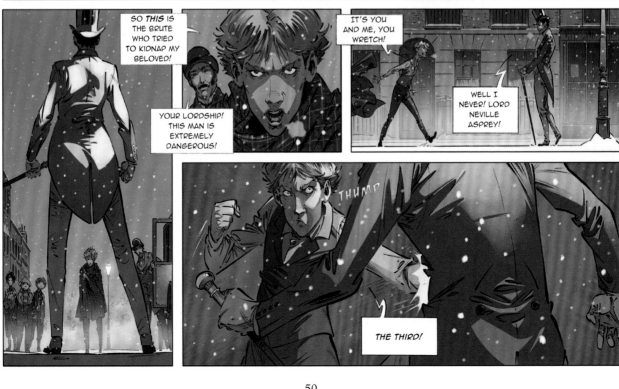

SO *THIS* IS THE BRUTE WHO TRIED TO KIDNAP MY BELOVED!

YOUR LORDSHIP! THIS MAN IS EXTREMELY DANGEROUS!

IT'S YOU AND ME, YOU WRETCH!

WELL I NEVER! LORD NEVILLE ASPREY!

THUMP

THE THIRD!

50

LOOK OUT! HE'S GOT A BLADE!

YOU'RE DEAD MEAT!

BLAM

DON'T MOVE, YOU SWINE! ANOTHER STEP AND I WILL NOT HESITATE TO SHOOT YOU LIKE THE RABID BEAST THAT YOU ARE!

YOU THINK YOU'RE A HERO, BUT YOU'RE TOO LATE, OLD MAN! MY MATE'S ALREADY UP THERE, DOING IN THE GIRL AND YOUR OLD LADY!

MARY!

GRACE!

GRACE!

MARY! GRACE! HOLD ON, WE'RE COMING!

MARY!

GENTLEMEN!

I'LL GET YOU, COPPER'S PUPPY!

WILLIAM FLETCHER, PERSONAL ASSISTANT TO MR. SHERLOCK HOLMES! THIS MAN'S A DANGEROUS CRIMINAL!

IF YOU HAVE HURT THEM, YOU FIEND, I SWEAR I'LL...

EVENING, WATSON!

MR. HOLMES?

CONGRATULATIONS, CHARLIE! YOU HAVE A BETTER EYE THAN OUR DEAR DOCTOR...

I SAY, WATSON, YOU SHOULD PUT YOUR GUN DOWN BEFORE YOU INJURE SOMEONE OR SHOOT YOURSELF IN THE FOOT!

NEVILLE?

JOHN?

HOLMES! IT'S YOU!

AH, AT LONG LAST...

PURR

?

LET ME GO, YOU CRETINS!

DON'T YOU KNOW WHO I AM?

MY NAME IS BLOODY PERCY! I WORK FOR HARRY SYKES! HARRY SYKES!

DON'T BOTHER, SON. YOU AIN'T IN THE EAST END NOW...

HEY!

INSPECTOR LESTRADE, WHAT A SURPRISE...

HARRY SYKES, YOU ARE UNDER ARREST.

THERE MUST BE SOME MISTAKE, INSPECTOR. I'M A RESPECTABLE BUSINESSMAN...

MY FOOT! YOU ARE A CROOKED EX-POLICEMAN WHO MOVED INTO RACKETEERING AND EXTORTION...SOON TO BE AN EX-EAST-END GANG BOSS. YOU'RE *FINISHED* THIS TIME.

STEADY ON, NOW. LET'S NOT GET CARRIED AWAY, INSPECTOR! IT'S PRETTY RISKY TO HURL SUCH ACCUSATIONS...

I HAVE THREE RELIABLE WITNESSES, INCLUDING THE MAN YOU KNEW BY THE NAME OF JASPER CRANE, WHOM YOU HIRED TO COMMIT A MURDER. IN ACTUAL FACT, HE WAS...AN UNDERCOVER DETECTIVE.

GENTLEMEN, HE IS ALL YOURS...

INTUITION NEVER WAS YOUR FORTE, HARRY, EVEN WHEN YOU WERE DISGRACING THE POLICE UNIFORM...

OH, I ALMOST FORGOT. I ALSO HAVE A STATEMENT FROM YOUR RIGHT-HAND MAN, BLOODY PERCY. TOOK HIM LESS THAN TEN MINUTES TO BETRAY YOU! WORTH SAVING HIM FROM THE GUTTER, WAS IT?

THANK YOU FOR THAT MOST COLORFUL ACCOUNT, BILLY FLETCHER!

MY BAKER STREET IRREGULARS, YOU ACTED LIKE TRUE PROFESSIONALS!

AND AS FOR DEAR OLD WATSON, WELL... HE WAS STUNNINGLY EFFECTIVE.

PRESUMABLY A MATTER OF MOTIVATION--HE ALWAYS WAS THE SENTIMENTAL TYPE.

BUT WHAT ABOUT YOU, SIR? HOW DID YOU GET MIXED UP IN ALL THIS?

"BELIEVE IT OR NOT, IT WAS A GENUINE COMBINATION OF CIRCUMSTANCES..."

"WHEN I ASSIGNED YOU TO OBSERVE HIS LORDSHIP, I HAD ABSOLUTELY NO IDEA THAT THIS MISSION WOULD LEAD YOU TO CROSS PATHS WITH HARRY SYKES AND HIS HENCHMEN..."

"...LET ALONE WITH ME!"

OBVIOUSLY IT DIDN'T TAKE ME LONG TO PICK UP THE TRAIL OF MY PREY--A PROFESSIONAL KILLER NAMED JASPER CRANE, A MAN AS CRAFTY AS HE WAS DANGEROUS...

"WITH THE HELP OF THE LOCAL POLICE, I HUNTED HIM DOWN INTO THE MAZE OF SEWERS..."

"WHEN WE FINALLY MET, ONLY MY MASTERY OF A JAPANESE SYSTEM OF WRESTLING ALLOWED ME TO SURVIVE."

ABOUT A YEAR AGO, THE MANCHESTER POLICE CALLED ME IN TO SOLVE A RATHER UNPLEASANT MURDER CASE. I'LL SPARE YOU THE DETAILS.

"IN THE CONFUSION, THE INSPECTOR WHO WAS ACCOMPANYING ME FIRED HIS GUN..."

"...THUS PUTTING AN END TO JASPER CRANE'S BLOODY CAREER."

"ON CLOSER EXAMINATION, I NOTICED HOW STRIKINGLY SIMILAR WE LOOKED..."

"AT MY REQUEST, CRANE'S DEATH WAS KEPT A SECRET. I HAD GAINED AN UNEXPECTED OPPORTUNITY TO INFILTRATE THE UPPER ECHELONS OF CRIME..."

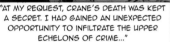

"WHEN I RETURNED TO LONDON, I BEGAN INTERMITTENTLY IMPERSONATING CRANE --ALLEGEDLY WISHING TO SET MYSELF UP IN THE EAST END AFTER NARROWLY ESCAPING THE MANCHESTER POLICE."

...AND STUMBLED UPON A FULLY ORGANIZED CRIMINAL CLIQUE...

UNDER THIS FALSE IDENTITY, I WAS ABLE TO MAKE NUMEROUS CONTACTS IN THE LONDON UNDERWORLD...

AND THAT'S HOW YOU ENDED UP BEING HIRED BY SYKES!

YOU HAVE THE MAKINGS OF A TRUE DETECTIVE, BILLY FLETCHER!

I HAD ALREADY MET SYKES A FEW TIMES WHILE POSING AS JASPER CRANE... SUCH AN INDIVIDUAL COULDN'T FAIL TO ESCAPE MY NOTICE, YET HE SEEMED UNTOUCHABLE; PROTECTED BY CORRUPTION AND A CODE OF SILENCE.

WHEN I LEARNED THAT HE WAS URGENTLY SEEKING A HIRED KILLER, I JUMPED AT THE CHANCE... AND THE REST YOU KNOW!

SO THAT WAS THE COMBI-THINGAMAJIG?

I'D CALL IT A **HUGE** STROKE O' LUCK.

GOOD EVENING, UNCLE. YOU AND I NEED TO HAVE A CONVERSATION.

BUT FIRSTLY, LET ME SAY THAT MY BRIEF SOJOURN IN YOUR DEBTOR'S ESTABLISHMENT HAS CLEARED MY HEAD.

I HAVE DONE SOME THINKING...

I AM DELIGHTED, MY BOY. NOW THAT YOU'VE COME TO YOUR SENSES, I HOPE YOU UNDER-STAND WHY I--

I'LL NEVER FORGIVE YOU AS LONG AS I LIVE! BUT I WISH TO DISCUSS SOMETHING COMPLETELY DIFFERENT...

...THE ONLY THING WHICH INTERESTS YOU--MONEY!

"I... I AM LISTENING..."

"HERE IS MY OFFER: YOU CAN HAVE IT ALL--THE PROPERTY, THE LAND, THE WHOLE FAMILY FORTUNE..."

"ALL I ASK IN RETURN IS THAT MY BETROTHED AND I BE KEPT FREE OF FINANCIAL WORRIES FOR THE REST OF OUR DAYS."

"WHAT? BUT..."

YOU WILL ALSO PROVIDE FUNDS TO REBUILD THE MUSIC HALL OF MR. CORBETT, MY FUTURE FATHER-IN-LAW.

"THERE. BESIDES THESE MINOR EXPENSES, WHICH YOU WILL PRESUMABLY ENDORSE, THE REST BELONGS TO YOU."

"COULD OUR LAWYERS HAVE THE NECESSARY PAPERS DRAWN UP BY THE END OF THE WEEK?"

"BUT... WHAT ABOUT YOUR POSITION IN SOCIETY?"

"I COULDN'T CARE LESS! IN CASE YOU FEAR MALICIOUS GOSSIP, REST ASSURED: GRACE AND I HAVE DECIDED TO LEAVE ENGLAND FOREVER, TO SETTLE IN ITALY--VENICE OR FLORENCE, PERHAPS... WE HAVE YET TO DECIDE."

"ER, NO DOUBT... BUT... YOUR MOTHER..."

TELL HER THAT I WILL WRITE, IF NEEDS BE, IF IT WILL AVERT ANOTHER FAINTING FIT.

OH, I SHALL LEAVE IT TO YOU TO EXPLAIN THE SITUATION TO HER. I'M SURE YOU WILL FIND THE RIGHT WORDS...

THERE YOU GO! I THINK WE WERE PRETTY FANTASTIC THIS TIME.

THANKS TO US, BLOODY PERCY, SYKES, AND THE WHOLE GANG ARE BEHIND BARS; LORD NEVILLE ASPREY WILL MARRY GRACE IN VENICE; AND MR. HOLMES...

KNOCK IT OFF, WOULD YA, BILLY FLETCHER?

OI, LADS! WHAT D'YA SAY TO BLOWIN' A BIT O' CASH? THEY SAY BENFORD'S MAKES AMAZIN' PIES...

PROFESSOR...

WHAT IS IT, COLONEL?

THE POLICE HAVE ARRESTED HARRY SYKES...AND HIS RIGHT-HAND MAN--YOU KNOW, SIR CHARLES ASPREY'S BASTARD... LESTRADE OF THE YARD IS IN CHARGE OF THE CASE. HE IS CURRENTLY DISMANTLING SYKES' ENTIRE ORGANIZATION...

THIS IS A MAJOR BLOW TO OUR INTERESTS IN THE EAST END! IT WAS YOU WHO VOUCHED FOR HIS COMPETENCE... I THOUGHT SYKES RULED THE WHOLE DISTRICT WITH AN IRON HAND?

THE FACT IS... APPARENTLY, SYKES WAS CAUGHT BY...AHEM... SHERLOCK HOLMES.

HOLMES!

ALL'S WELL THAT ENDS WELL!

END OF CHAPTER 3

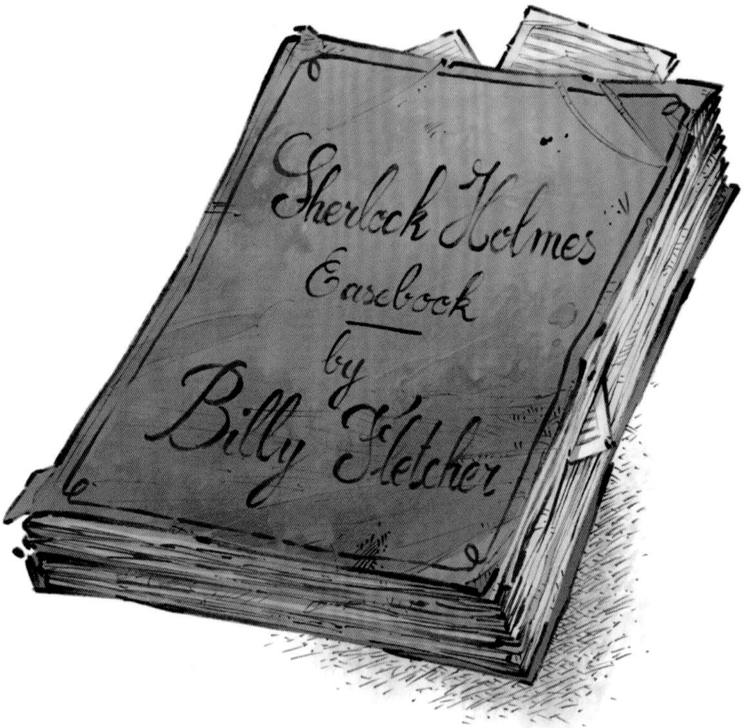
Sherlock Holmes
Casebook
by
Billy Fletcher

The Orphans of London

SHERLOCK HOLMES IS DEAD!

IT CAN'T BE TRUE...

WHAT HAPPENED? WHAT ARE THEY SAYIN'?

WELL, THAT... THAT MR. HOLMES...FELL OFF SOME KIND OF PRECIPICE OR WATERFALL. I DON'T REALLY UNDERSTAND.

A PLACE CALLED THE REICHEN— SOMETHING FALLS... IN THE MOUNTAINS... IN SWITZERLAND...

WHERE'S THAT?

HOW D'YA MEAN, "FELL"?

IT... IT SAYS HE WAS FIGHTING WITH...

...WITH PROFESSOR MORIARTY...AND THEY FELL INTO THAT DAMNED WATERFALL TOGETHER...

MORIARTY?

AIN'T THAT THE FELLA HE TALKED ABOUT BEFORE?

HE'S HIS ARCH-ENEMY! THE NAPOLEON OF CRIME! MR. HOLMES MENTIONED HIM SEVERAL TIMES! HAVE YOU FORGOTTEN THE CASE OF THE MERRY MINSTREL AND BLOODY PERCY?

OH, RIGHT, IT'S COMIN' BACK NOW... SORRY, BILLY FLETCHER, I AIN'T SUCH A SWOT AS YOU...

HEY, THAT'LL DO!

TOM! LEAVE HIM BE, WILL YA?

SO HOLMES IS DEAD... MAY HE REST IN PEACE AND ALL, BUT WHAT CAN WE DO ABOUT IT?

AS THEY SAY, LIFE GOES ON...

JUST HAVE TO FIND ANOTHER SCHEME, THAT'S ALL...

ARE YOU GONNA SHUT UP?

OH YEAH, AND WHY SHOULD I, NOW?

MR. HOLMES WAS MORE THAN A BOSS!

HE WAS OUR MENTOR! BUT YOU STILL DON'T KNOW WHAT THAT MEANS, RIGHT? YOU ILLITERATE IRISHMAN!

YOU'RE WRONG, CLEVER CLOGS! IT MEANS YA THOUGHT HE WAS YER DADDY! IT'S COMMON FER BOYS WHO NEVER KNEW THEIR FATHERS...

CUT IT OUT!

STOP IT!

ARE YOU MAD, TOM? YA CAN'T SAY THAT!

62

KEEP OUT O' THIS! I AIN'T HAVIN' SOME *GIRL* TELLIN' ME WHAT TO DO!

GO CHEER UP HOLMES JUNIOR INSTEAD... ME, I'M OFF! I'VE HAD IT UP TO HERE WITH CRYBABIES AND GIRLIES!

BE SEEIN' YOUS, GANG! BLACK TOM'S GOIN' BACK TO *KILBURN!*

THAT'S IT! GET LOST, YA DIRTY QUITTER! AND DON'T COUNT ON US TO HELP NEXT TIME YOU'RE IN TROUBLE!

ALRIGHT, BILLY?

LEAVE ME ALONE!

NO WAY, OL' MAN... I'M UPSET ABOUT MR. HOLMES TOO, YA KNOW... I WAS ALSO...

LEAVE ME ALONE, I SAID! I DON'T NEED YOU! I DON'T NEED ANYONE, YOU HEAR?! 'SPECIALLY NOT A GIRL! CAN'T YOU SEE IT'S ALL OVER, NOW THAT...HE'S DEAD?

BILLY, WAIT...

FORGET IT! WHY DON'T YOU GO AND LOOK AFTER YOUR MAD MUM IN BEDLAM?! SHE PROBABLY NEEDS YOU!

NO POINT IN US KNOCKING AROUND TOGETHER!

IT'S THE END OF THE BAKER STREET IRREGULARS!

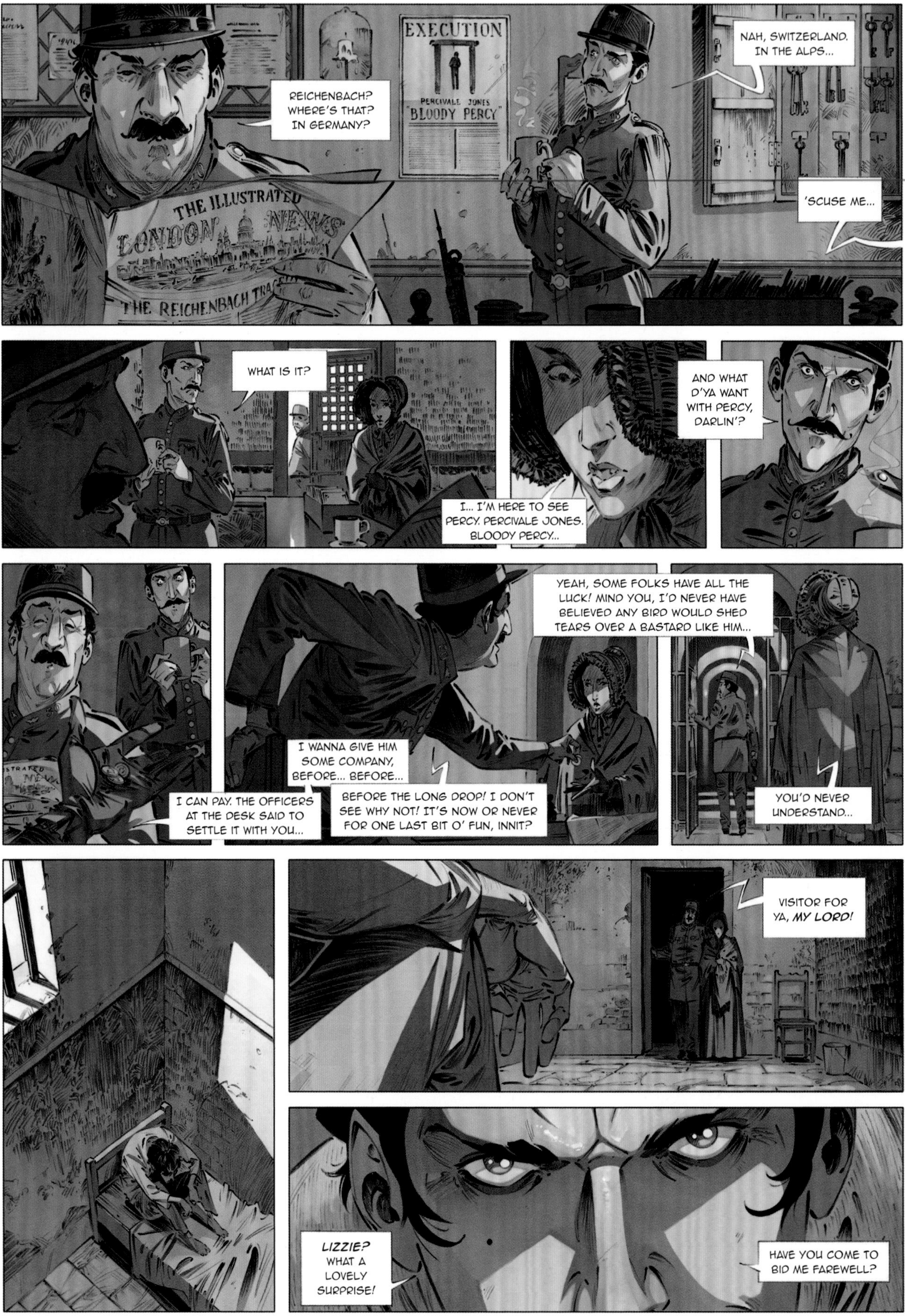
EXECUTION
PERCIVALE JONES
"BLOODY PERCY"
THE ILLUSTRATED LONDON NEWS
THE REICHENBACH TRA
REICHENBACH? WHERE'S THAT? IN GERMANY?
NAH, SWITZERLAND. IN THE ALPS...
'SCUSE ME...
WHAT IS IT?
I... I'M HERE TO SEE PERCY. PERCIVALE JONES. BLOODY PERCY...
AND WHAT D'YA WANT WITH PERCY, DARLIN'?
I WANNA GIVE HIM SOME COMPANY, BEFORE... BEFORE...
I CAN PAY. THE OFFICERS AT THE DESK SAID TO SETTLE IT WITH YOU...
BEFORE THE LONG DROP! I DON'T SEE WHY NOT! IT'S NOW OR NEVER FOR ONE LAST BIT O' FUN, INNIT?
YEAH, SOME FOLKS HAVE ALL THE LUCK! MIND YOU, I'D NEVER HAVE BELIEVED ANY BIRD WOULD SHED TEARS OVER A BASTARD LIKE HIM...
YOU'D NEVER UNDERSTAND...
VISITOR FOR YA, *MY LORD!*
LIZZIE? WHAT A LOVELY SURPRISE!
HAVE YOU COME TO BID ME FAREWELL?

STOP SNIVELING! SO, DID SCABS AND HIS BOYS EXPLAIN EVERYTHING?

YEAH, BUT... ABOUT ME LI'L GIRL... THEY... THEY WON'T HARM HER, WILL THEY? SHE'LL BE ALRIGHT, EH?

I'LL LEAVE YA TO IT... JUST KNOCK WHEN YOU'VE DONE YER BUSINESS... SEE YA SOON, LOVEBIRDS!

YOU HAVE MY WORD AS A GENTLEMAN, LIZZIE... RIGHT, HURRY UP! THERE'S NO TIME FOR CHATTER...

FEEL FREE TO COME BACK ONCE WE'VE HANGED THAT SCUMBAG, DARLIN'!

US LOT NEEDS A BIT O' COMPANY, TOO, SOMETIMES...

THAT'S IT THEN, ME DEAR WATSON! NO MORE INVESTIGATIN' FOR MR. HOLMES, AFTERNOON TEA AT BAKER STREET. IT'S ALL OVER...

US TWO WILL HAVE TO GET BY ON OUR OWN NOW...

IT'S A PITY. WE REALLY WAS A GOOD TEAM...

OH, I AIN'T SO WORRIED ABOUT TOM. RIGHT NOW, I BET HE'S ALREADY BACK WITH HIS COUSINS IN KILBURN. I'M SURE THEY WELCOMED HIM WITH OPEN ARMS. A BURGLAR OF HIS CALIBER, 'COURSE THEY DID...

NAH, IT'S BILLY I'M WORRIED ABOUT THE MOST, YA SEE...

SO THE SWISS AUTHORITIES STILL HAVE NOT FOUND THE BODIES?

NOT TO MY KNOWLEDGE. LISTEN, INSPECTOR, THANK YOU KINDLY FOR YOUR CONDOLENCES, BUT I'VE JUST GOT BACK FROM THE CONTINENT, AND I SHOULD LIKE TO--

I UNDERSTAND, DR. WATSON. I ALSO HAVE THINGS TO DO... BUT I BEAR MORE BAD NEWS...

WHAT IS IT?

BLOODY PERCY HAS ESCAPED... TWO DAYS AGO. I'VE PUT ALL MY MEN ON IT.

ESCAPED? BUT HOW?

THAT MATTERS LITTLE. CONSIDERING THE THREATS HE MADE WHEN HE WAS ARRESTED, WE FEEL THERE IS A STRONG CHANCE HE WILL TRY TO GET EVEN AND ATTACK YOU...

...OR MY WIFE. I SEE! WHAT DO YOU SUGGEST?

AS SOON AS I HEARD THE NEWS, I POSTED SEVERAL OF MY MEN NEAR YOUR HOME. I WANTED TO WARN YOU, IN CASE YOU NOTICE THEM...

MRS. WATSON AND YOURSELF CAN RELY ON OUR PROTECTION, DOCTOR.

AND THE IRREGULARS?

I BEG YOUR PARDON?

THE BAKER STREET IRREGULARS... THE STREET CHILDREN WHO HELPED US CATCH THAT SWINE... HE THREATENED TO KILL THEM, TOO--HAVE YOU FORGOTTEN?

OH, THEM! NOT TO WORRY, DR. WATSON!

THEY'LL MANAGE ON THEIR OWN... THEY'RE USED TO IT, ARE THEY NOT? ANYHOW, HER MAJESTY'S POLICE HAS OTHER THINGS TO DO.

APPARENTLY... GOOD DAY, INSPECTOR.

WHAT? THAT'S ALL YOUS MANAGED TO PINCH IN AN AFTERNOON'S WORK?

ANYONE'D THINK I NEVER TAUGHT YOUS NOTHIN'... OR YOUS WANTED TO HURT YER POOR MAM!

AND WHERE'S SHE GOT TO NOW, BY THE WAY?

HERE I AM, PADDY MALONE, AND LOOK WHO I'VE BROUGHT!

BY ALL THAT'S HOLY! IF IT AIN'T THAT BAD SEED TOM O'ROURKE!

YOUS REMEMBER YER COUSIN TOM, LADS?

HELLO, RORY...

I'M BARRY. HE'S RORY.

HELLO, TOM!

RIGHT, YOU'RE STAYIN' FER DINNER! YA MUST HAVE HEAPS TO TELL US AFTER SO LONG!

WELL, I MEAN... YEAH... AND, IN FACT, I'D LIKE TO STAY AROUND A WHILE LONGER...

MAKE YERSELF AT HOME, TOM! FAMILY'S SACRED...'SPECIALLY IN HARD TIMES! AIN'T THAT SO, LADS?

HERE, MY BOY! COMIN' RIGHT UP!

ER, THANKS, AUNTIE CAIT...

AH, HERE'S OUR PRINCESS!

HELLO, COUSIN TOM!

YA REMEMBER *KITTY*, TOM? SEE HOW SHE'S GROWN?

69

WELL?

THE AREA'S CRAWLIN' WITH COPPERS... BUT THERE IS SOME GOOD NEWS!

WE SPOTTED ONE OF HOLMES'S LI'L SNEAKS...

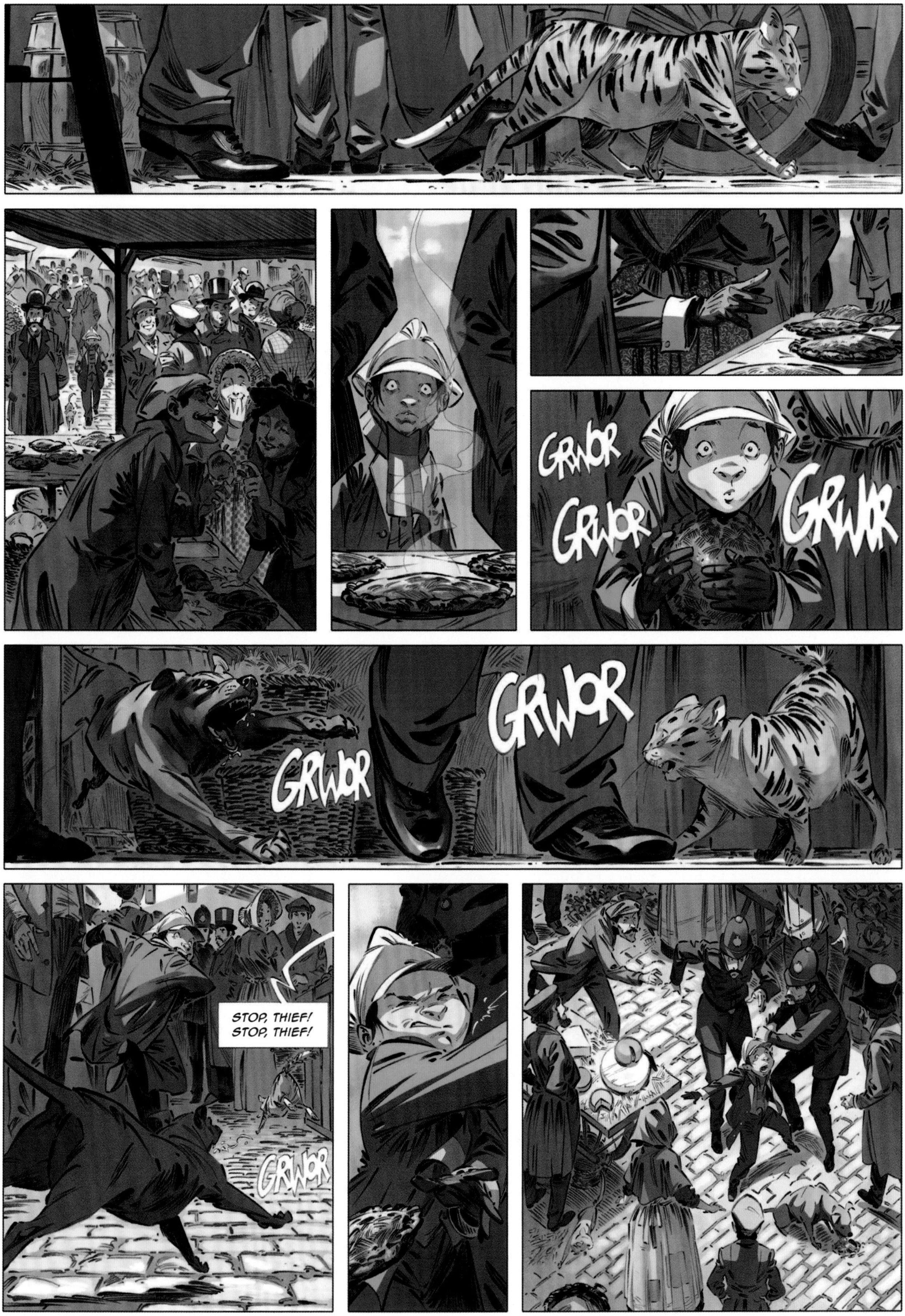
GRWOR
GRWOR
GRWOR
GRWOR
GRWOR
STOP, THIEF!
STOP, THIEF!
GRWOR

RIGHT, LADS, NO MORE AMATEUR JOBS NOW THAT YER COUSIN'S HERE! TOM'S A REAL ROOF-CAT! NOW, WE'LL BE ABLE TO TURN OVER A FEW HOUSES IN LA-DI-DAH DISTRICTS...

TOM, YOU'LL GO FIRST: SLIP INSIDE QUIETLY WITH THE TWINS AND HELP YERSELF TO THE SILVERWARE, NICE AND QUICK-LIKE, WHILE JIMMY'S ON LOOKOUT!

THE MAIN THING'S TO SHARE OUT THE TASKS: EV'RYONE IN ON THIS HAS A PART TO PLAY! RORY, BARRY, AND JIMMY, YOU'RE IN CHARGE O' LOOKIN' THE PLACES OVER...

?

TWO OR THREE JOBS LIKE THAT... AND WE'RE SET UP FER LIFE!

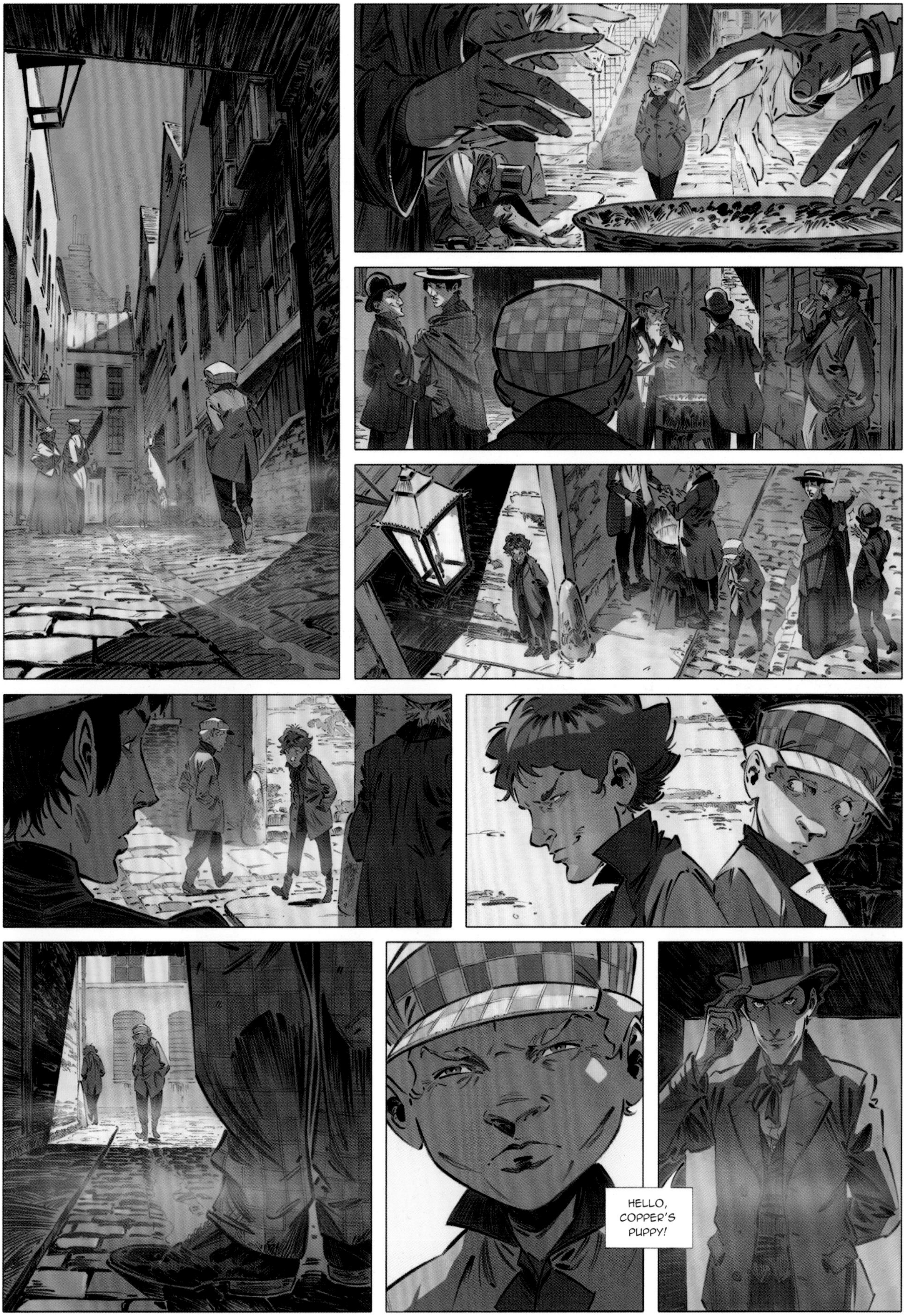
HELLO, COPPER'S PUPPY!

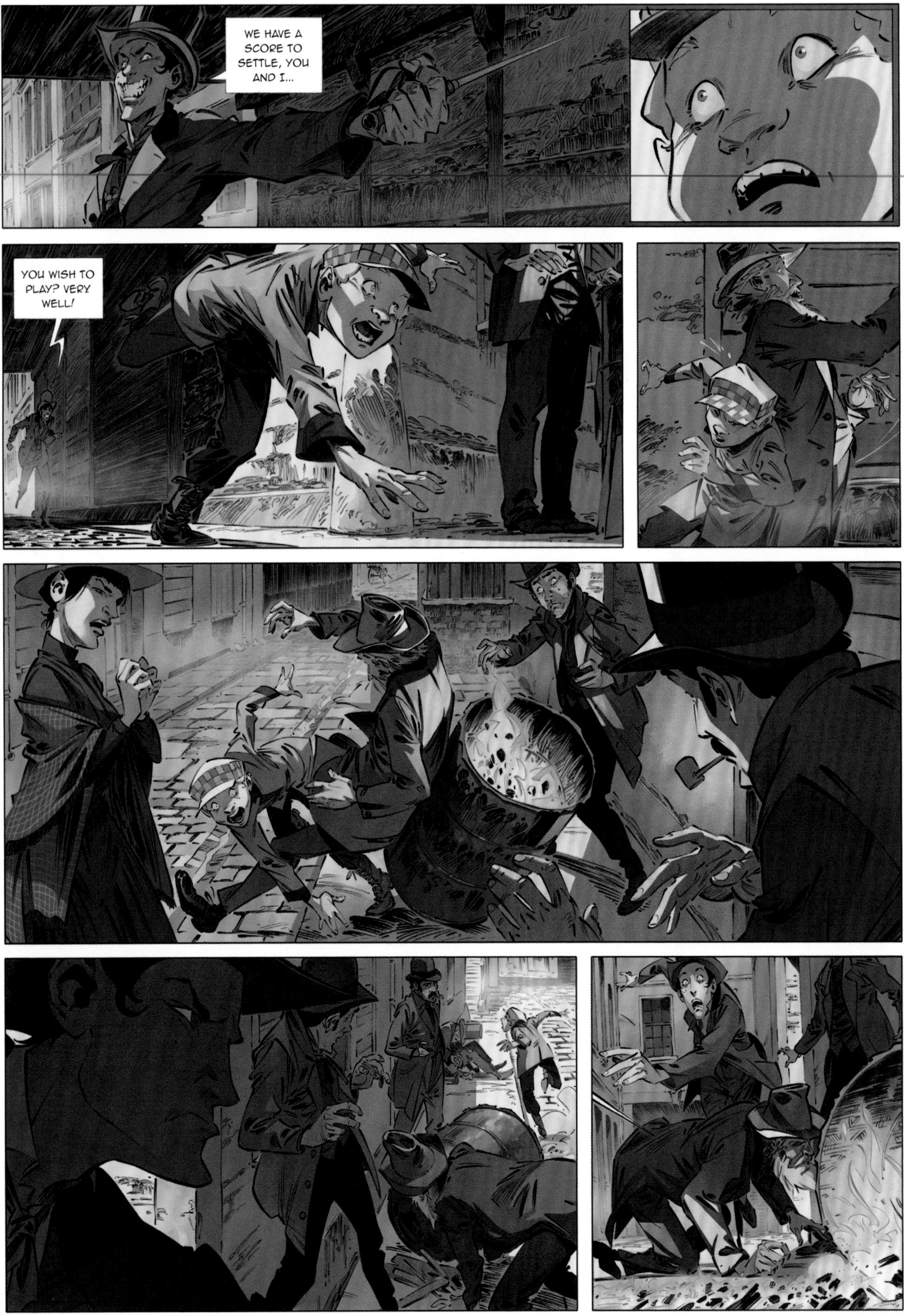
WE HAVE A SCORE TO SETTLE, YOU AND I...
YOU WISH TO PLAY? VERY WELL!

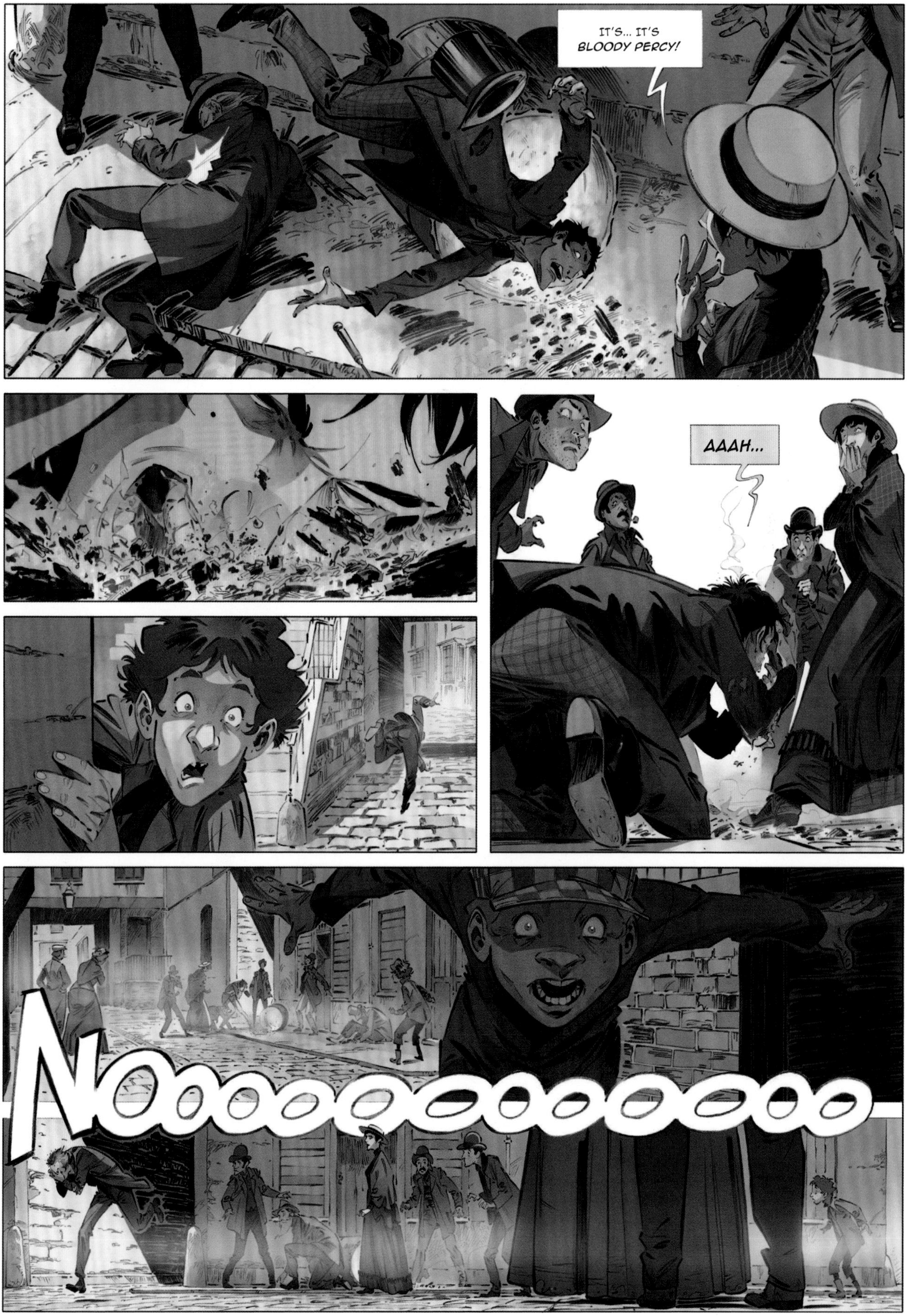
IT'S... IT'S BLOODY PERCY!
AAAH...
NOOOOOOOOOOOOO

RULES & ORDERS

WHAT YOU HAVE DONE IS VERY WICKED, MY CHILD... DON'T YOU KNOW THE EIGHTH COMMANDMENT? *THOU SHALT NOT STEAL!*

BUT OF COURSE IT ISN'T ENTIRELY YOUR FAULT. YOU GREW UP ON THE STREETS, AMID THE RIFFRAFF, SCORNING THE LAW AND FORGETTING GOD...

BUT OUR LORD HAS NOT FORGOTTEN YOU!

IN HIS INFINITE MERCY, HE WILLED HUMAN JUSTICE TO BE LENIENT AND TO COMMIT YOU INTO MY CARE AND THAT OF *MISS CAVENDISH.*

God is truth

WE'LL TAME YOU HERE, MY GIRL!

"IN THIS HOUSE, WE ENDEAVOR TO PUT LOST SHEEP AND YOUNG, DAMNED SOULS BACK ON THE STRAIGHT AND NARROW...

"HOW? THROUGH PRAYER AND WORK, FOR THE DEVIL MAKES WORK FOR IDLE HANDS!

"YES INDEED, MY CHILD, IT IS DIVINE PROVIDENCE THAT BROUGHT YOU HERE TO US. YOU SHALL ATONE FOR YOUR SINS, TEMPER YOUR SOUL, AND MAKE YOURSELF USEFUL TO SOCIETY AT LAST. SO, ER... CHARLOTTE, IS IT?"

PARISH WORKHOUSE

THE NAME'S *CHARLIE!*

76

THIS IS THE LAUNDRY. YOU WILL WORK IN HERE.

CHILDREN, THIS IS OUR NEW RESIDENT. HER NAME IS CHARLOTTE.

THE NAME'S *CHARLIE!*

SWASH

HER NAME IS *CHARLOTTE*, AND, AS YOU CAN SEE, SHE'S ANOTHER INSOLENT PIECE OF WORK! BUT SHE'LL SOON REALIZE WHERE SHE IS!

YOU! SEE TO IT THAT LITTLE MISS INSOLENT GETS DOWN TO WORK, FAST! AND YOU LOT, STOP LAZING AROUND!

HORRID OL' BAG!

WHAT'S YER NAME?

DUNNO, I FORGOT...

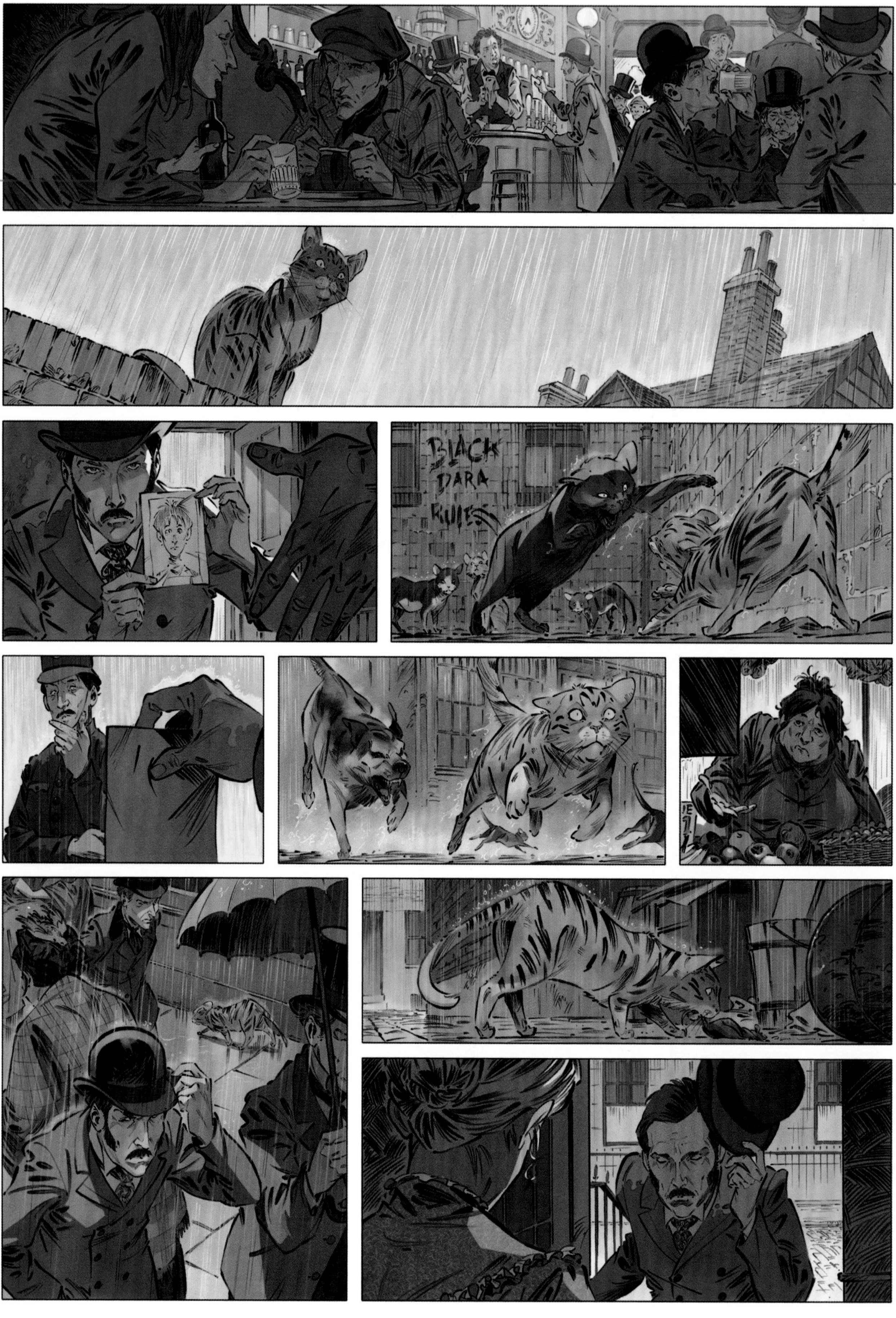
BLACK
DARA
RULES

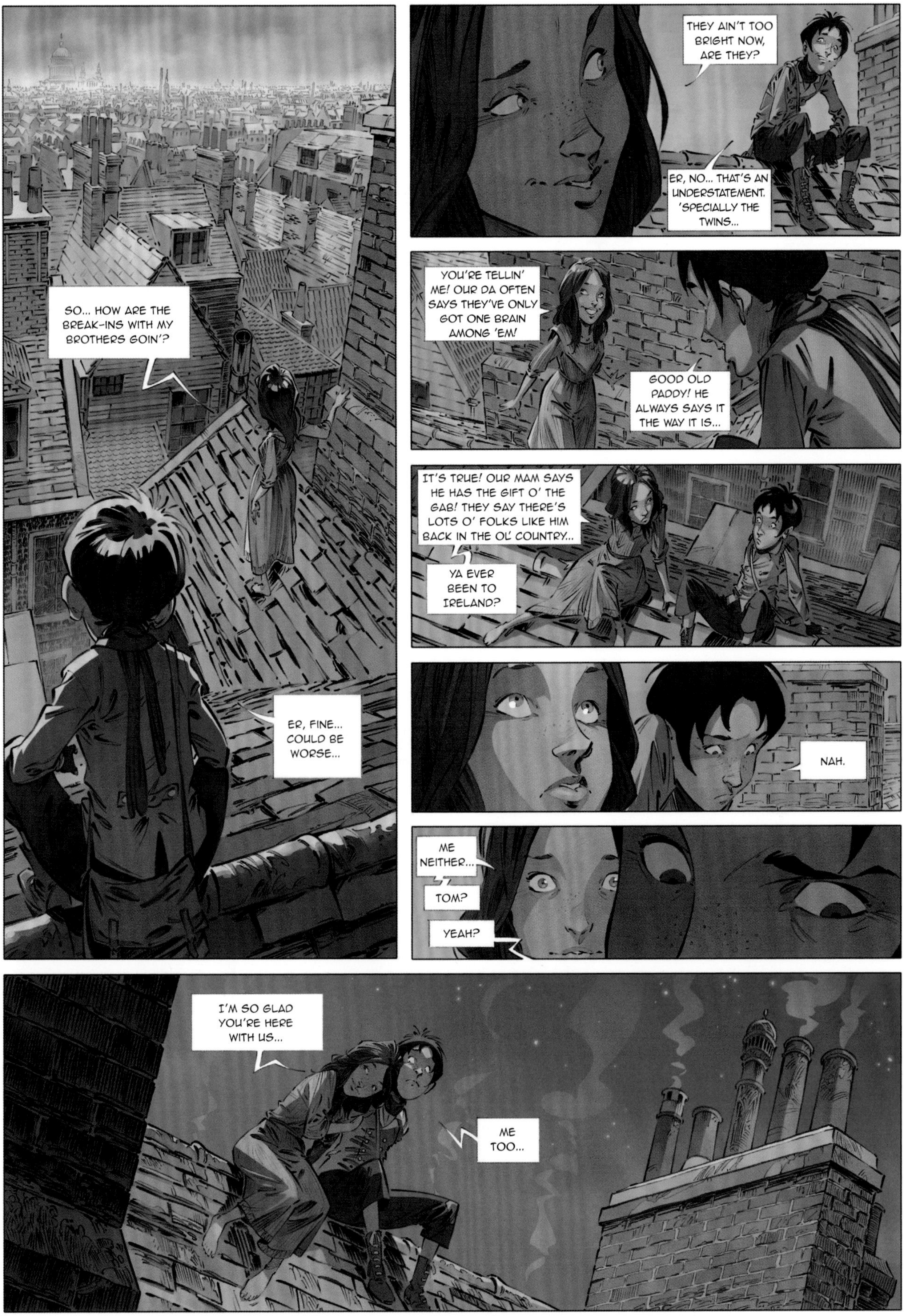
SO... HOW ARE THE BREAK-INS WITH MY BROTHERS GOIN'?
ER, FINE... COULD BE WORSE...
THEY AIN'T TOO BRIGHT NOW, ARE THEY?
ER, NO... THAT'S AN UNDERSTATEMENT. 'SPECIALLY THE TWINS...
YOU'RE TELLIN' ME! OUR DA OFTEN SAYS THEY'VE ONLY GOT ONE BRAIN AMONG 'EM!
GOOD OLD PADDY! HE ALWAYS SAYS IT THE WAY IT IS...
IT'S TRUE! OUR MAM SAYS HE HAS THE GIFT O' THE GAB! THEY SAY THERE'S LOTS O' FOLKS LIKE HIM BACK IN THE OL' COUNTRY...
YA EVER BEEN TO IRELAND?
NAH.
ME NEITHER...
TOM?
YEAH?
I'M SO GLAD YOU'RE HERE WITH US...
ME TOO...

DOCTOR WATSON!

BILLY FLETCHER! I'VE LOOKED EVERYWHERE FOR YOU AND YOUR FRIENDS! WHERE ARE TOM AND CHARLIE?

THAT'S JUST IT-- I HAVE NO IDEA... I'M LOOKING FOR THEM, TOO.

WE... WE HAD A ROW ABOUT...MR. HOLMES'S DEATH, AND I HAVEN'T HEARD FROM THEM SINCE...

BUT WE ABSOLUTELY MUST FIND THEM... TO WARN THEM THAT... ER, I DON'T KNOW IF YOU'RE AWARE, BUT...

...BLOODY PERCY'S ESCAPED, AND HE'S AFTER US!

LET'S GO AND LOOK FOR CHARLIE AND TOM TOGETHER, MY BOY, AND WE'LL SURELY FIND THEM!

BUT BEFORE THAT, DO COME UP FOR A NICE HOT MEAL AND--

SO YOU WANT US TO BE A TEAM? LIKE... LIKE IT WAS WITH MR. HOLMES?

LIKE IT WAS WITH MR. HOLMES, BILLY...

THE BAKER STREET IRREGULARS ARE FAR FROM BEATEN YET!

OI, NEW GIRL!

YEAH, AND WE'RE GONNA EXPLAIN...

SHE SAYS YOU'RE A REBEL... THEY'RE ALL LIKE THAT AT FIRST, BUT THEY SOON LEARNS HOW FINGS WORK IN HERE!

YA NEEDN'T BOTHER. I DON'T PLAN ON STAYIN'...

IS THAT SO?! WELL, MEANWHILE, IT'S LIKE THIS: FROM NOW ON, YA GIVES US HALF O' YER MEALS...

UNLESS YOU'RE LOOKIN' FOR TROUBLE...

YOU'RE WASTIN' YER TIME, AND IF YA KEEP ON HARASSIN' ME, IT'S YOU WHO'LL BE IN TROUBLE...

DID YOU HEAR THAT, NELLY?!

WHO DOES SHE FINK SHE IS?

THINK YA CAN MAKE TROUBLE FOR *ME?!*

I USED TO WORK FOR SHERLOCK HOLMES! THAT NAME RING A BELL?

RECKON A COUPLA DODOS LIKE YOU CAN SCARE ME, DO YA?!

OH YEAH, I FORGOT--ME MUM'S WITH THE LOONIES IN BEDLAM. MUST RUN IN THE FAMILY!

NO ONE'S EVER STOOD UP TO 'EM LIKE YOU DID.

YOU OUGHTA BEWARE O' THEM TWO, YA KNOW...

NELLY ONCE STUCK A GIRL'S HEAD INTO--

I DON'T CARE! SO, WHAT'S YER NAME?

ROSIE.

CHEERS FOR YER HELP, ROSIE.

IS IT TRUE WHAT YA TOLD 'EM?

THAT ME MUM'S IN BEDLAM? YEAH...

NAH, THAT YA WORKED FOR SHERLOCK HOLMES.

YEAH...

WITH ME MATES, A WHILE BACK...

82

YOU'RE STRAININ' YERSELVES FER NAUGHT, INSPECTOR. AIN'T NOTHIN' HERE...

OH, I'M SURE, MALONE... I WAS JUST PASSING BY AND DROPPED IN TO SAY HELLO. I KNOW YOU'VE ALREADY FENCED OFF THE LOOT BY NOW.

WHO IS YOUR FENCE, BY THE WAY? OLD MAN MCGOWAN? EDDIE THE JEWELS?

THIS IS ALL 'COS WE'RE IRISH!

I'VE NO IDEA WHAT YOU'RE ON ABOUT, INSPECTOR...

BUT NO, 'COURSE NOT! IT'S EASIER TO COME RANSACKIN' HONEST WORKERS' HOMES!

AIN'T YOUS GOT NOTHIN' BETTER TO DO? WHY AREN'T YOUS OUT CHASIN' THAT KILLER WHAT RAN AWAY? PERCY WHATSISNAME...

KNOCK IT OFF, CAIT MALONE, UNLESS YOU WANT TO GO TO JAIL...

NOT TO WORRY, KIDS! YER MAM'S HERE!

YEAH, MUMMY'S HERE TO PLAY MOTHER HEN... UNTIL YOU ALL LAND UP IN THE WORKHOUSE WHEN YOUR DADDY'S SCHEMES MISFIRE!

WE'VE FOUND TWO MORE, INSPECTOR!

THEY WERE CANOODLING ON THE ROOF...

RUBBISH!

GET OFF ME, YA BRUTE!

NOT GOT HER WALKING THE STREETS YET? SHE'D BE EVER SO POPULAR...

SO, HERE'S THE GIRL OF THE HOUSE! KITTY, IS IT? YOU'RE A PRETTY ONE...

NO ONE TOUCHES A HAIR ON HER HEAD WHILE I'M ALIVE!

LEAVE IT, DA! HE JUST WANTS YA TO SLAP HIM SO HE CAN SEND YA TO JAIL, BUT HE AIN'T WORTH IT!

OHO! SHE'S A *SMART* ONE, TOO!

AND WHO'S THIS BLACKHEAD? A DISTANT COUSIN?

YEAH. THAT A PROBLEM?

THE IRISH ARE LIKE BLOODY RABBITS IN A MAGIC SHOW--THERE'S ALWAYS ONE MORE POPPING OUT OF THE HAT...

THAT'S A PRETTY CRUMMY METAPHOR!

MY, WHAT A CLEVER LITTLE POPINJAY! WHERE DID YOU PICK UP A WORD LIKE THAT, SCUM? DON'T TELL ME YOU CAN READ!

RIGHT! THIS ISN'T OVER. SEE YOU SOON, PADDY. WE MAY DROP BY AGAIN... MEANWHILE, YOU SHOULD HAVE YOUR MISSUS TIDY UP THE PARLOR A LITTLE. IT'S A MESS IN HERE...

HE'LL NEVER LEAVE US BE... THAT BRADDOCK'S A REAL BULLDOG!

MIGHT BE A GOOD IDEA TO STOP THE BREAK-INS, PADDY, TILL THINGS'VE CALMED DOWN...

IT'S ALL A LOAD O' COPPER CLAPTRAP!

LIKE THE POET SAID: *THE BULLDOGS GOT THE BARK, BUT THE IRISH GOT THE LUCK!* AIN'T THAT SO, LADS?

"MEDAFFER"... HONESTLY, TOM, WHERE'D YA GET A WORD LIKE THAT?

A BRAINY...FRIEND O' MINE TAUGHT IT TO ME. HE COULD READ AND ALL. BUT IT'S *METAPHOR*.

FER EXAMPLE, IF A GIRL HAS GREEN EYES, AND YA SAY SHE'S GOT EMERALDS IN HER GAZE--THAT'S A METAPHOR, LIKE...

WHAT'S IT MEAN? SOUNDS LIKE SOME DISEASE...

IT'S A KIND O' SYMBOL. AN IMAGE... BUT IN WORDS. FER EXAMPLE...

YES?

TOM! WE NEED TO TALK ABOUT OUR NEXT JOB! AND KITTY, GO HELP YER MAM TIDY UP, INSTEAD O' PRATTLIN' ON!

...AND YOU'RE *SURE* IT WAS BLOODY PERCY?

YES, INDUBITABLY.

OHO! OUR YOUNG FRIEND HAS QUITE A VOCABULARY!

THIS IS CRUCIAL EVIDENCE, INSPECTOR!

SOMEONE WITH A BURNED FACE STANDS OUT--EVEN IN THE EAST END.

I KNOW THAT YOUR MEN ARE TERRIBLE OBSERVERS, BUT...

WELL NOW, DOCTOR! STARTING TO TALK LIKE MR. HOLMES, ARE YOU?

WE DO MISS HIM, OF COURSE...

WE ABSOLUTELY MUST FIND YOUR FRIENDS BEFORE THEY BUMP INTO BLOODY PERCY.

TOM HAS FAMILY DOWN KILBURN WAY... PERHAPS WE SHOULD START THERE?

AS FOR CHARLIE, I'VE NO IDEA WHERE SHE MIGHT GO. HER MUM'S IN BEDLAM, AND WE WERE HER ONLY FAMILY...

SERIOUSLY, I THOUGHT WE WAS ALL **GONERS** THAT TIME!

YA SHOULDA SEEN BILLY AND TOM RUNNIN' LIKE THE CLAPPERS, AND THEM LOONIES AFTER US...

SO THEN I PULLS OUT ME SLINGSHOT AND--

ALRIGHT, ROSIE?

IT'S NUFFIN'... THINK I CAUGHT A COLD YESTERDAY... IT'LL GO... FINISH YER STORY...

KOFF KOFF

LISTEN, ROSIE... I'M GONNA ESCAPE SOON...

BUT THERE'S NO WAY...OUT OF HERE...

RUBBISH! ME, TOM, AND BILLY GOT A GENTLEMAN OUT O' BEDLAM ONCE! THAT WAS ANOTHER STORY, TRUST ME!

KOF KOF

I'VE GOT A PLAN... WE'LL WAIT TILL YA FEEL BETTER, AND THEN WE CAN BOTH GET AWAY FROM HERE!

WHAT D'YA SAY TO THAT?

KOF KOF

OUTTA ME WAY, DODOS!

WELL! LITTLE MISS INSOLENT! HAVE YOU NOTHING TO DO AT THE LAUNDRY?

I'M GOIN' BACK... BUT YOU'VE GOTTA DO SOMETHIN' FOR ROSIE! SHE'S REALLY POORLY. SHE WON'T STOP COUGHIN', AND--

LISTEN, WILL YA?! ROSIE'S UNWELL!

WHAT DO YOU EXPECT ME TO DO? AND IT'S NO REASON TO STOP WORKING! GO BACK IMMEDIATELY!

YOU'VE GOTTA CALL HER A DOCTOR! I KNOW ONE; HIS NAME'S DR. WAT--

SWASHH!

NOW WILL YA LOOK AT THAT! WHAT'S IT WORTH, D'YA THINK?

A FORTUNE! THESE TOFFS ARE RIGHT IDIOTS! LEAVIN' ALL THIS BEHIND TO GO OFF INTO THE COUNTRY... JUST ASKIN' FER TROUBLE, AIN'T THEY?!

RIGHT, THAT'S ENOUGH O' THAT, LADS! WE NEED TO GO, NOW!

WAIT! THERE'S STILL TONS O' STUFF!

SHUT UP! I HEARD A NOISE...

QUIT FRETTIN'! ANYHOW, JIMMY'S--

POLICE! DON'T MOVE!

CAUGHT YOU RED-HANDED!

SO, YOU KILBURN BASTARDS! SAID I'D NICK YOU, DIDN'T I?

89

BOSS! THE BLACK-HEAD'S RUNNING OFF!

TOMPKINS! WITH ME!

SO, BURGLAR BOY, THINK YOU KNOW ALL THE TRICKS, EH?!

YEAH!

WHAK

90

SO YOU'RE GOING BACK TO THOSE...HORRIBLE PLACES?

DON'T FORGET YOU'RE SPEAKING TO A FORMER SOLDIER OF HER MAJESTY, MY DEAR! LONDON CAN'T BE WORSE THAN AFGHANISTAN, CAN IT NOW?

ALL I HOPE IS THAT WE FIND TOM AND CHARLIE BEFORE BLOODY PERCY DOES.

WHEN I THINK THAT MONSTER COULD BE HOLED UP A FEW STREETS AWAY, I... I FEEL SO TERRIBLY NERVOUS, JOHN.

POOR CHILDREN! BUT WHAT CAN WE DO, JOHN?

I AM GOING TO HELP BILLY LOOK FOR HIS FRIENDS... AFTER ALL THEY DID FOR HOLMES, IT'S THE LEAST I CAN DO.

"LESTRADE'S MEN ARE WATCHING THE AREA AROUND THE CLOCK."

"IF BLOODY PERCY DECIDES TO COME PROWLING AROUND HERE, THEY WILL ARREST HIM ON THE SPOT."

"BUT WHAT ABOUT YOU, JOHN? WHAT IF YOU CROSS PATHS DURING YOUR...INVESTIGATIONS?"

DON'T YOU WORRY, MARY. I'LL BE CAREFUL... AND ARMED.

KOF
KOF

ROSIE...

WELL? DID THEY CALL A DOCTOR?

KOFF
KOFF

NAH... MISS CAVENDISH...MADE ME DRINK SOME NASTY STUFF... AND THE REVEREND...CAME TO SEE ME... SAID IT'D GET BETTER BY TOMORROW...

GONNA TELL ME... ABOUT YER PLAN, THEN?

KOFF
KOFF

YEAH... IT CAN'T FAIL...

DURIN' MORNIN' BREAK, YA KNOW, WHEN THE HOSPITAL GEEZERS COME FOR THEIR LAUNDRY BASKETS...

YEAH...

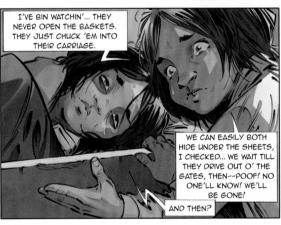

I'VE BIN WATCHIN'... THEY NEVER OPEN THE BASKETS. THEY JUST CHUCK 'EM INTO THEIR CARRIAGE.

WE CAN EASILY BOTH HIDE UNDER THE SHEETS, I CHECKED... WE WAIT TILL THEY DRIVE OUT O' THE GATES, THEN--POOF! NO ONE'LL KNOW! WE'LL BE GONE!

AND THEN?

KOF KOF

THEN WE'LL GET BY! I'VE BIN LIVIN' ON THE STREETS SINCE I WAS A NIPPER, YA KNOW... I'LL SORT THINGS OUT, YOU'LL SEE!

WHAT'S THAT WHISPERING OVER THERE? IS IT YOU AGAIN, LITTLE MISS INSOLENT?

CHARLIE... LEAVE! GET AWAY BEFORE... BEFORE YA CATCH YER DEATH, LIKE ME...

LET GO O' ME, YA BUNCH OF ENGLISH BASTARDS!

GET YER FILTHY HANDS *OFF*, I TELL YA! WE'VE DONE NOTHIN'!

DON'T WASTE YOUR BREATH... YOUR THREE BRATS ARE ALREADY IN JAIL. THEIR NUMBER'S UP, AND SO'S YOURS--*YOU'LL NEVER SEE THEM AGAIN!*

MY DAUGHTER... SHE'S NOTHIN' TO DO WITH ALL THIS. I SWEAR IT...

RIGHT, PADDY? TELL 'EM! SAY SOMETHIN', FER GOD'S SAKE! YA CAN'T LET 'EM CART HER OFF!

RIGHT, NO MORE JOKES! TAKE THIS SCUM AWAY!

THAT'S SIX MORE IRISH LOCKED UP!

WE COULDN'T FIND HIM... HE AIN'T IN HIS HIDEOUT, AND NOBODY'S SEEN HIM AROUND.

BUT WE BROUGHT YA SOME FOOD AND DRINK... WE THOUGHT--

AND THE OTHER TWO? THE GIRL AND THE BLACKHEAD?

SAME FING! THEY MUSTA SCARPERED TOO...

THIS IS GETTIN' RISKY, PERCY... IF THE BLOND ONE BLABBED TO THE COPPERS, P'RAPS WE SHOULD--

I WANT THOSE THREE BRATS DEAD, D'YOU HEAR, SCABS? THE BLOND ONE, THE BLACKHEAD, AND THE GIRL! I'LL MAKE 'EM BLEED! I WANNA WATCH 'EM DIE AT MY FEET!

YOU AND THE BOYS GO HANG AROUND THE BLOND ONE'S HIDEOUT. COME AND TELL ME THE **SECOND** ONE OF THE BASTARDS SHOWS UP... *GOT IT?*

I GET IT.

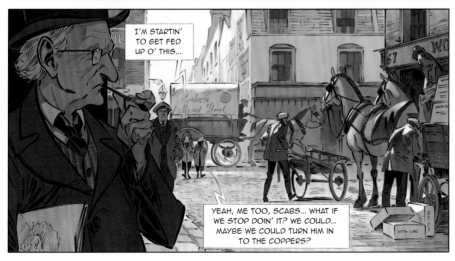

I'M STARTIN' TO GET FED UP O' THIS...

YEAH, ME TOO, SCABS... WHAT IF WE STOP DOIN' IT? WE COULD... MAYBE WE COULD TURN HIM IN TO THE COPPERS?

NO ONE'S TALKIN' TO THE COPPERS, THAT CLEAR?! AND YOU SHUT YER BIG MOUTH IF YA DON'T WANNA WIND UP IN THE RIVER WITH THE FISHES... *GOT IT?*

I GET IT.

WE ARE WASTING OUR TIME... THESE PEOPLE WON'T TELL US ANYTHING.

YES... AND I DON'T THINK WE SHOULD STAY HERE.

WE AIN'T TOO KEEN ON QUESTIONS 'ROUND HERE...

'SPECIALLY IF IT'S THE ENGLISH ASKIN' 'EM...

I ADVISE YOU TO CHANGE YOUR TONE, YOUNG FELLOW!

YEAH! THIS AIN'T NO PLACE FER YOUS...

TOO RIGHT, FRIEND! *GET LOST*, YA BRITS!

CAN YA BELIEVE HOW THIS TOFF'S TALKIN'? RIGHT, LET'S SHOW HIM HOW WE DO THINGS IN KILBURN...

YA'LL SHOW NOTHIN' AT ALL, RODDY MCSHANE!

UNLESS YA WANT ME TO KICK YER ARSE IN FRONT O' YER GOOD-FER-NOTHIN' MATES...

MAM, WE'RE BUSY WITH SOMETHIN' HERE...

YEAH, SO I SEE... SOMETHIN' THAT'LL BRING THE COPPERS BACK 'ROUND HERE! AIN'T WE SEEN ENOUGH OF 'EM TODAY? WANNA END UP LIKE THE MALONES, D'YA?

COPPERS BUSTED IN HERE THIS MORNIN' AND CARTED OFF A WHOLE FAMILY. THEY WAS AFTER THE SAME KID YOU'RE LOOKIN' FER, TOO. DIDN'T GET HIM THOUGH. HE RAN AWAY...

AND YA'D DO THE SAME, IF YOUS HAD ANY GUMPTION!

...FOR OUR LORD, IN HIS INFINITE KINDNESS, CHOSE TO OFFER LOST SOULS REDEMPTION...

LOOKIN' FOR YER MATE? SO YOU AIN'T HEARD, THEN?

...BUT THE PATH TO SALVATION IS ROCKY AND STREWN WITH TRIALS, FOR SIN...

HEARD WHAT?

SHE'S DEAD. THEY'RE CARTIN' HER OFF NOW.

YEAH... P'RAPS YA THOUGHT SHE WAS HAVIN' A LIE-IN?

YOU AGAIN?!

ROSIE! IS IT TRUE THAT SHE'S DEAD?

98

AND THAT'S ALL YOU'VE GOT TO SAY, *YOU OL' BAG?!*

INDEED, THE LORD HAS CALLED HER HOME. SHE WAS OF RATHER A FRAIL CONSTITUTION, POOR THING...

SLUASH

GOD IS JUST

WELL? HOW DOES IT FEEL?

CLAC

STOP HER!

99

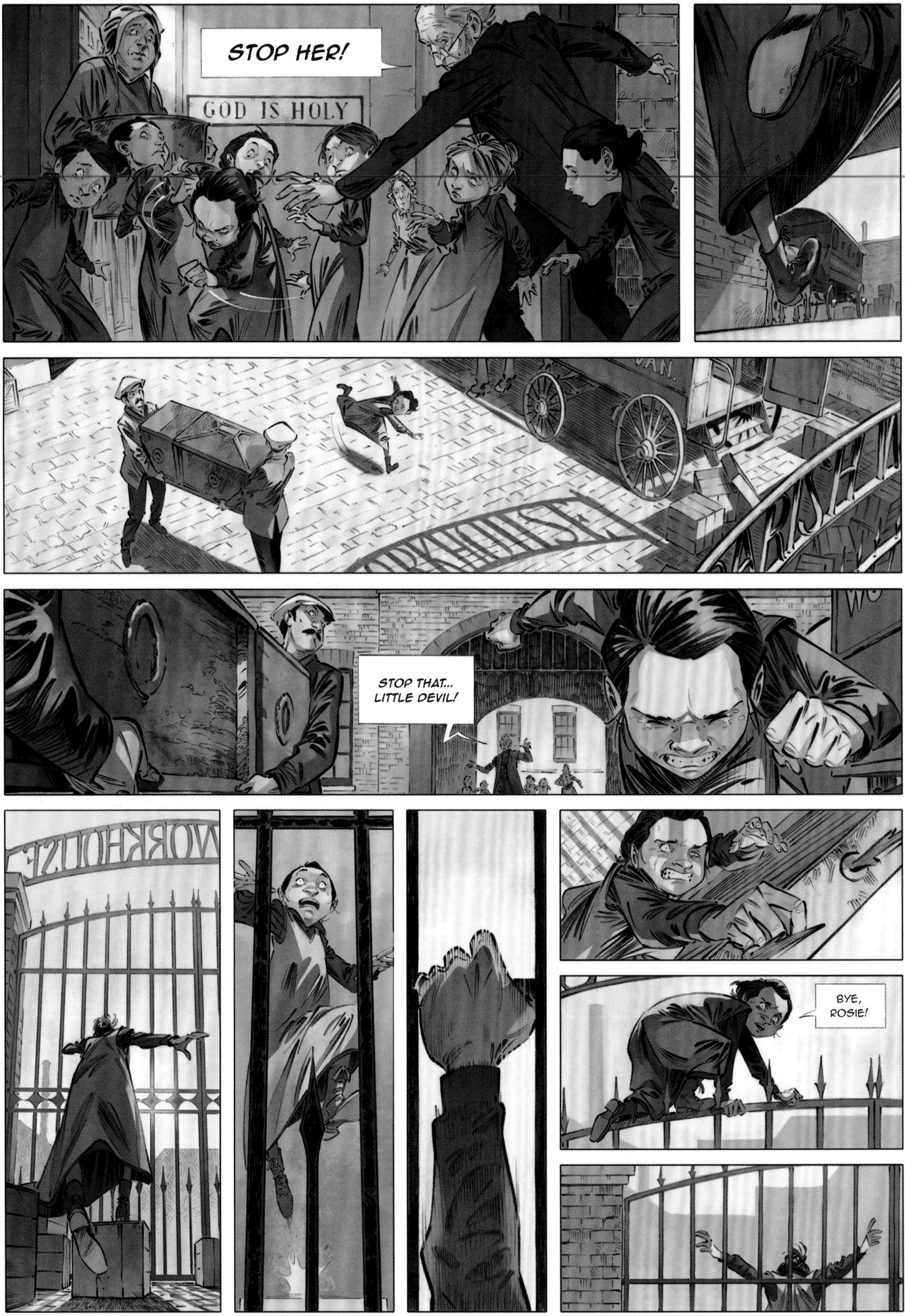
STOP HER!
GOD IS HOLY
STOP THAT... LITTLE DEVIL!
WORKHOUSE
BYE, ROSIE!

ARE YOU QUITE SURE THAT YOU WOULDN'T LIKE TO SLEEP HERE, BILLY? AS WE SAID, IT IS NO TROUBLE AT ALL...

THANKS VERY MUCH, MA'AM, BUT I NEED TO GET BACK TO OUR HIDEOUT, IN CASE TOM TURNS UP. AND SINCE HE'S GOT THE COPPERS ON HIS A...

AHEM... YES, YOUNG TOM IS... TEMPORARILY AT ODDS WITH THE POLICE.

TAKE CARE OF YOURSELF, BILLY, AND LET US KNOW WHAT HAPPENS!

101

"A DETECTIVE'S MAIN ASSET IS A KEEN EYE, MY DEAR BILLY! MOST PEOPLE ARE CONTENT TO LOOK BUT ARE UNABLE TO OBSERVE..."

A TRUE DETECTIVE MUST BE ABLE TO CALL ON HIS VISUAL MEMORY AT ALL TIMES...

"...SO THAT, IN CRITICAL MOMENTS, HE CAN FIT ALL THE PIECES OF THE PUZZLE TOGETHER, AS OUR DEAR WATSON WOULD SAY!"

IT WAS THE GIRL, I TELL YA! I RECOGNIZED HER!

BUT PERCY SAID SHE WAS DRESSED LIKE A BLOKE!

YOU TWO STAY HERE! I'M OFF TO FETCH PERCY!

BUT IT WAS HER, I SWEAR!

WHY WOULD SHE GO INTO THEIR BLOODY HIDEOUT IF IT WEREN'T HER?

SEE THAT? LOOKS LIKE PERCY'S GONNA KILL TWO BIRDS WITH ONE STONE...

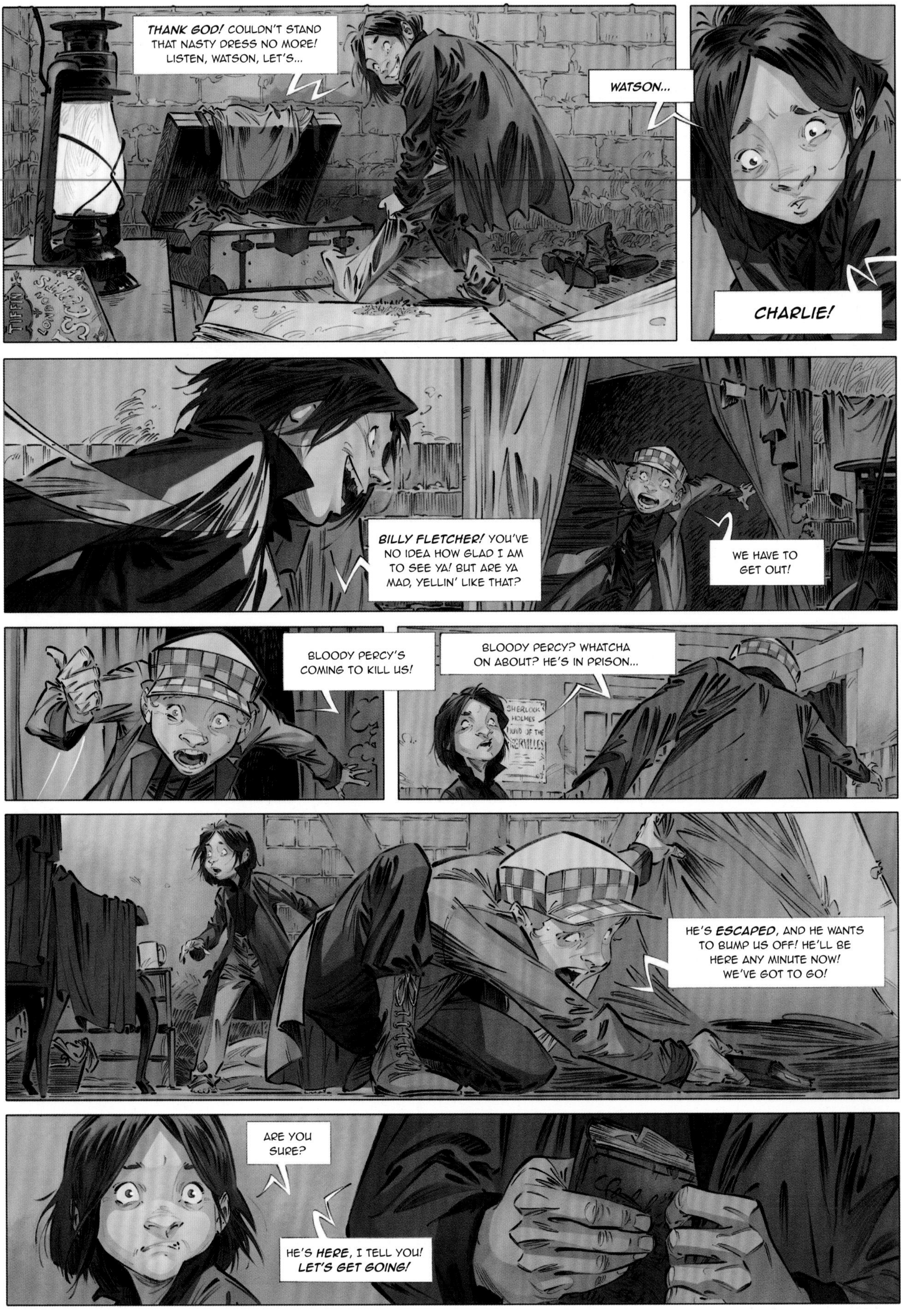
THANK GOD! COULDN'T STAND THAT NASTY DRESS NO MORE! LISTEN, WATSON, LET'S...
WATSON...
CHARLIE!
BILLY FLETCHER! YOU'VE NO IDEA HOW GLAD I AM TO SEE YA! BUT ARE YA MAD, YELLIN' LIKE THAT?
WE HAVE TO GET OUT!
BLOODY PERCY'S COMING TO KILL US!
BLOODY PERCY? WHATCHA ON ABOUT? HE'S IN PRISON...
SHERLOCK HOLMES
HOUND OF THE
HE'S ESCAPED, AND HE WANTS TO BUMP US OFF! HE'LL BE HERE ANY MINUTE NOW! WE'VE GOT TO GO!
ARE YOU SURE?
HE'S HERE, I TELL YOU! LET'S GET GOING!

SO, YOU SNEAKS!

HAPPY TO SEE ME?

DIRTY BASTARDS!

I'M COMING, YOU RATS!

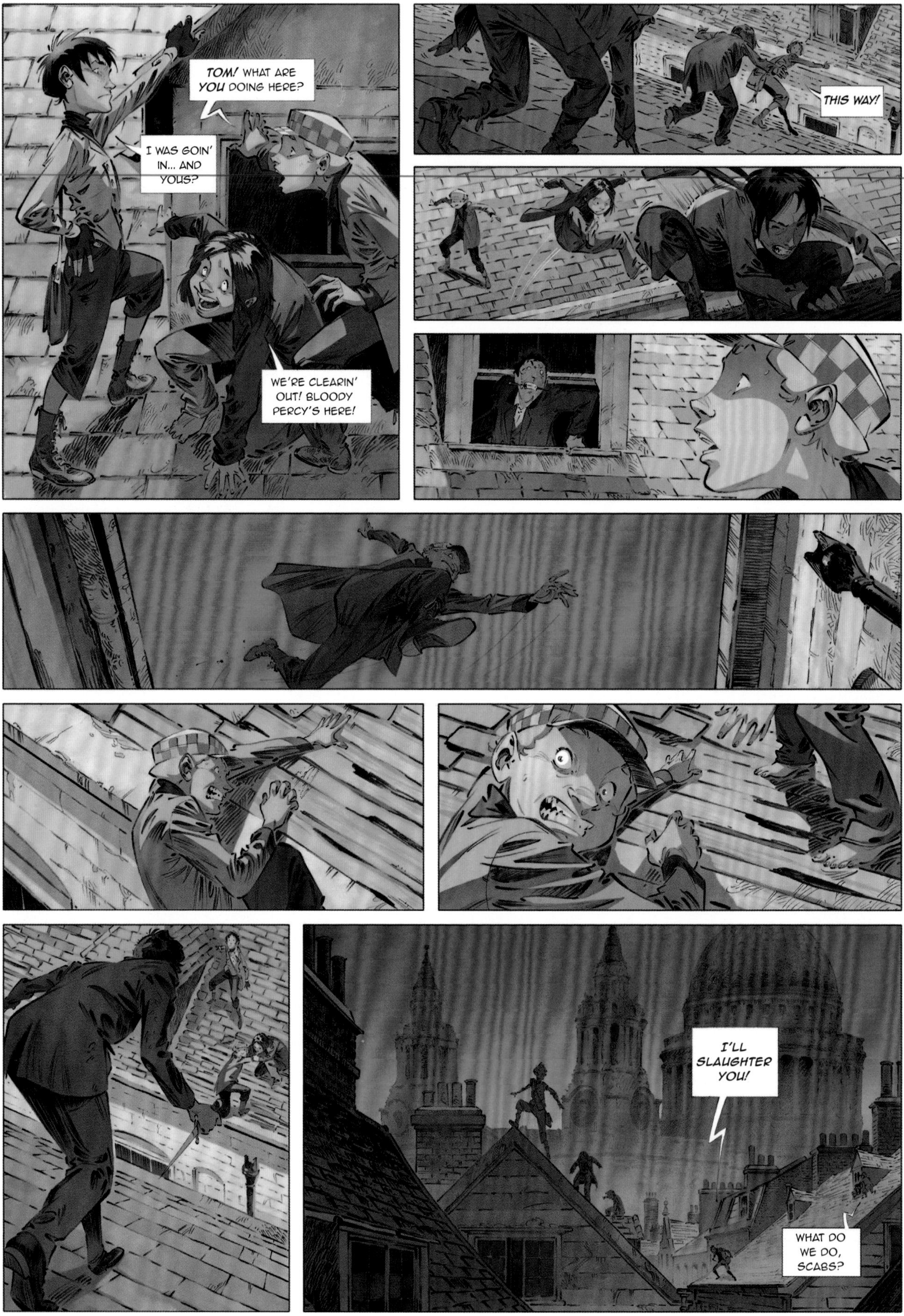
TOM! WHAT ARE YOU DOING HERE?
I WAS GOIN' IN... AND YOUS?
WE'RE CLEARIN' OUT! BLOODY PERCY'S HERE!
THIS WAY!
I'LL SLAUGHTER YOU!
WHAT DO WE DO, SCABS?

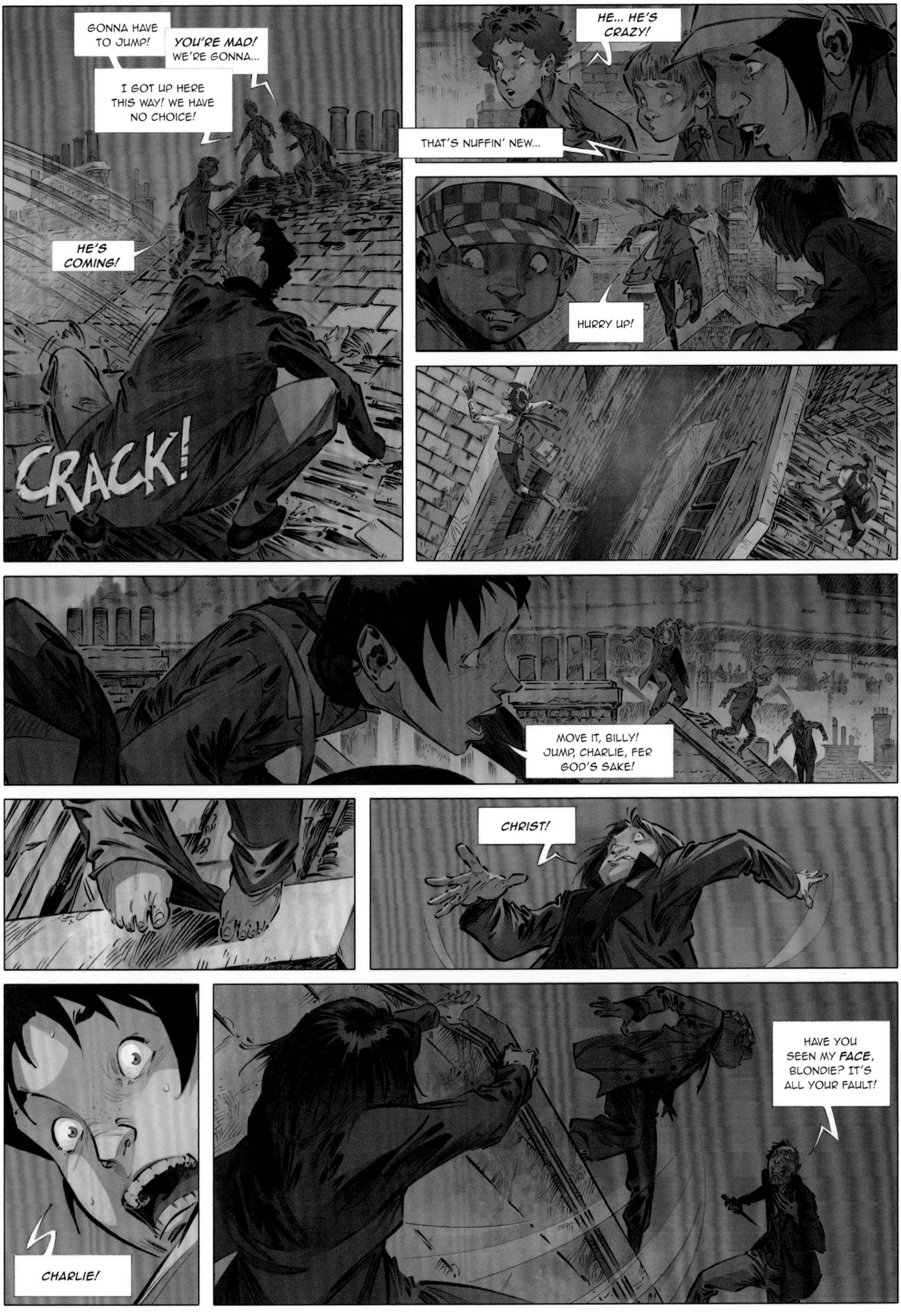
GONNA HAVE TO JUMP!
YOU'RE MAD! WE'RE GONNA...
I GOT UP HERE THIS WAY! WE HAVE NO CHOICE!
HE'S COMING!
CRACK!
HE... HE'S CRAZY!
THAT'S NUFFIN' NEW...
HURRY UP!
MOVE IT, BILLY! JUMP, CHARLIE, FER GOD'S SAKE!
CHRIST!
CHARLIE!
HAVE YOU SEEN MY FACE, BLONDIE? IT'S ALL YOUR FAULT!

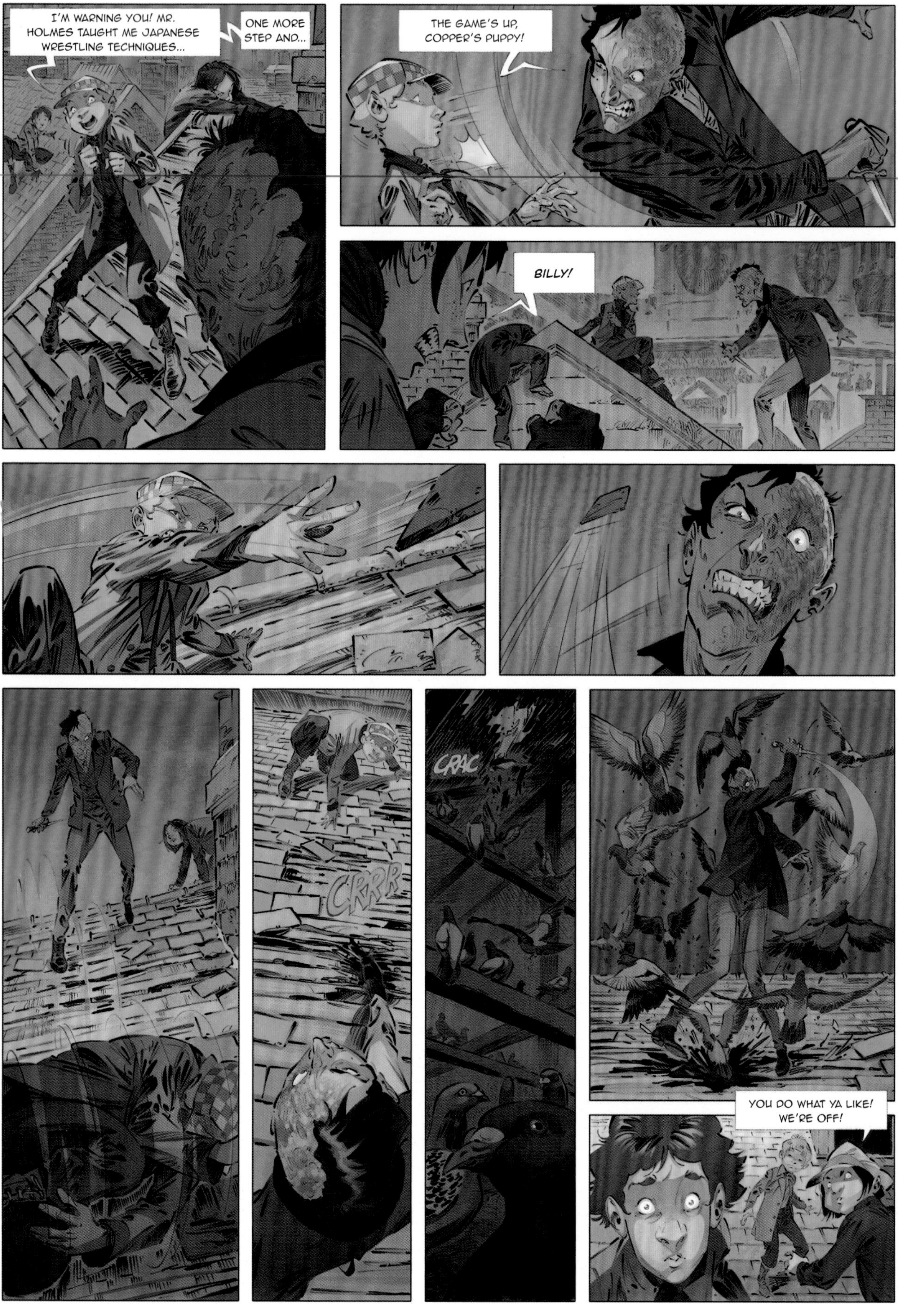
I'M WARNING YOU! MR. HOLMES TAUGHT ME JAPANESE WRESTLING TECHNIQUES...
ONE MORE STEP AND...
THE GAME'S UP, COPPER'S PUPPY!
BILLY!
CRAC
CRRR
YOU DO WHAT YA LIKE! WE'RE OFF!

BILLY! LOOK OUT!

HUMFF!

BILLY! NO!

AND NOW IT'S TIME FOR THE GIRL...

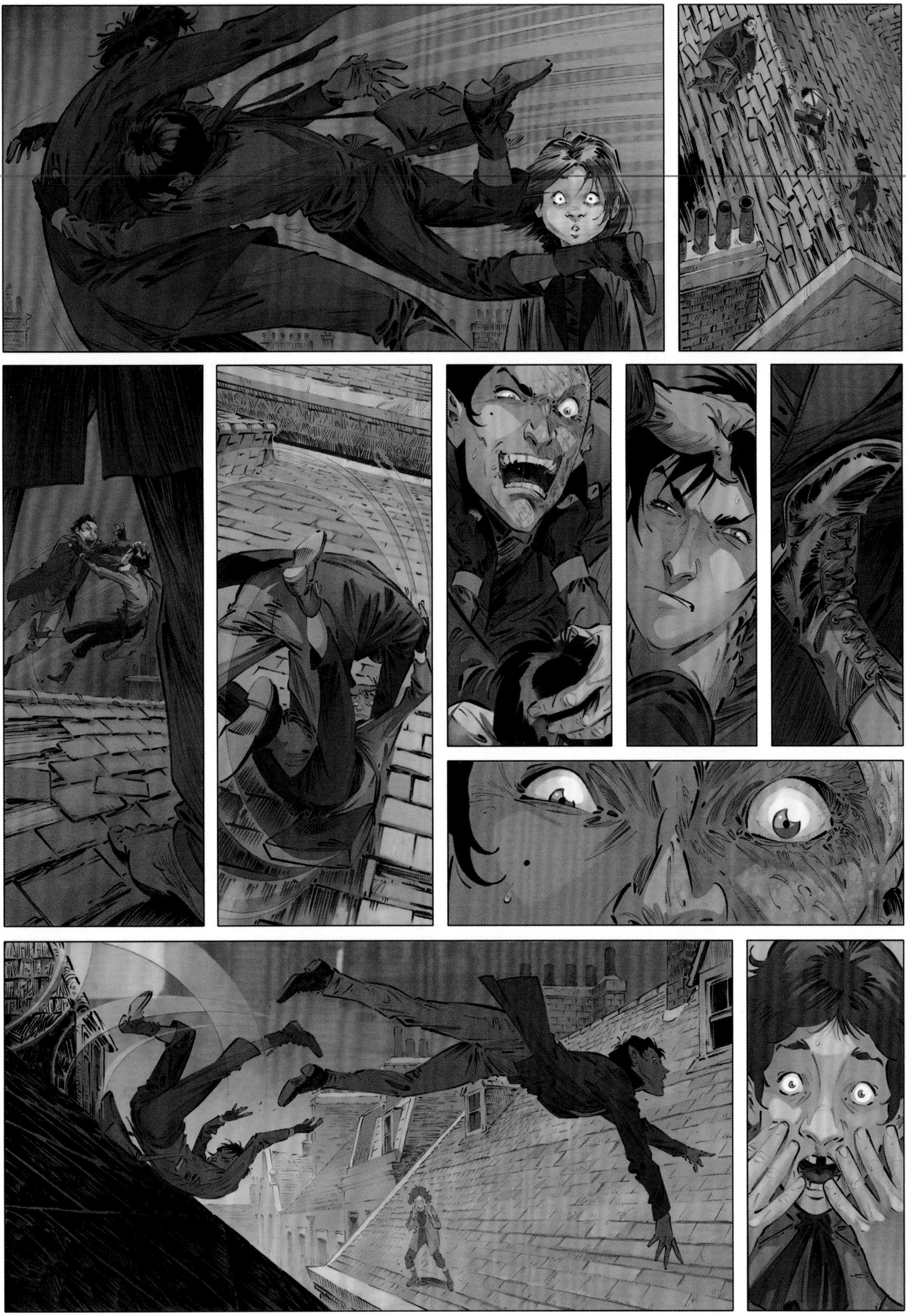

BILLY!

BILLY FLETCHER... YA LUCKY DEVIL!

YEAH... SAVED BY MR. HOLMES...

AND BLACK TOM O' KILBURN, TOO!

TOM, BILLY, CHARLOTTE! YOU HAVE A VISITOR!

MRS. HUDSON!

HELLO, CHILDREN!

I BROUGHT SOMEONE WHO--

WATSON!

BUT HOW DID YOU FIND HIM?

IT WAS RATHER HE WHO FOUND ME! IT'S AS IF HE WERE MISSING BAKER STREET...

BUT I'D SAY HE'S FORGOTTEN ME ALREADY...

CHEERS FOR TAKIN' CARE OF HIM, MA'AM... I DUNNO WHAT TO SAY...

YOU CALLED YOUR CAT... WATSON?

WELL, DOCTOR, ALL'S WELL THAT ENDS WELL.

YES, I SUPPOSE SO. I MUST ADMIT, I AM RELIEVED TO BE RID OF BLOODY PERCY ONCE AND FOR ALL.

BUT I WORRY ABOUT OUR YOUNG FRIENDS. CHILDREN SHOULD NEVER BE FORCED TO LIVE SUCH LIVES.

PROBABLY... BUT WHAT CAN WE DO? YOU KNOW AS WELL AS I DO--THEY COULD BE MUCH WORSE OFF...

HONESTLY, LESTRADE, I WONDER HOW YOU CAN REMAIN SO INSENSITIVE TO--

OH, BY THE WAY...

I SPOKE TO BRADDOCK THE BULL-DOG, MY COLLEAGUE FROM KILBURN. I PERSUADED HIM TO FORGET A "BLOODY IRISH BLACKHEAD" WHO SLIPPED THROUGH HIS FINGERS.

REALLY? BUT HOW?

BRADDOCK DREAMS OF JOINING SPECIAL BRANCH. I PROMISED TO PUT IN A GOOD WORD FOR HIM AT THE TOP. HE'LL SOON HAVE OTHER FISH TO FRY, AND OTHER IRISH TO NICK...

LESTRADE, I DON'T KNOW HOW...

SAY NO MORE, DOCTOR. LET'S JUST SAY I DID IT IN MEMORY OF MR. HOLMES. AS FOR OUR YOUNG FRIENDS...

"...THEY'LL JUST HAVE TO MANAGE ON THEIR OWN FROM NOW ON..."

MR. HOLMES?

THERE'S A LETTER FOR YOU, SIR...

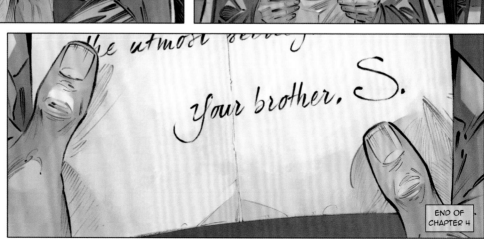

END OF CHAPTER 4

www.insightcomics.com

Find us on Facebook:
www.facebook.com/InsightEditionsComics

Follow us on Twitter:
@InsightComics

Follow us on Instagram:
Insight_Comics

Original Title: Les Quatre de Baker Street vol. 3
Authors: J.B. Djian, Olivier Legrand, David Etien

© Editions Glénat 2011– ALL RIGHTS RESERVED

Original Title: Les Quatre de Baker Street vol. 4
Authors: J.B. Djian, Olivier Legrand, David Etien

© Editions Glénat 2012 – ALL RIGHTS RESERVED

Library of Congress Cataloging-in-Publication Data available.

ISBN: 978-1-68383-019-1

Publisher: Raoul Goff
Associate Publisher: Vanessa Lopez
Senior Editor: Mark Irwin
Managing Editor: Alan Kaplan
Art Director: Chrissy Kwasnik
Production Editor: Elaine Ou
Production Manager: Alix Nicholaeff

 ROOTS of PEACE  REPLANTED PAPER

Insight Editions, in association with Roots of Peace, will plant two trees for each tree used in the manufacturing of this book. Roots of Peace is an internationally renowned humanitarian organization dedicated to eradicating land mines worldwide and converting war-torn lands into productive farms and wildlife habitats. Roots of Peace will plant two million fruit and nut trees in Afghanistan and provide farmers there with the skills and support necessary for sustainable land use.

Manufactured in Hong Kong by Insight Editions

10 9 8 7 6 5 4 3 2 1